W9-CON-638

WILLIAM LYON MACKENZIE

Rebel Against Authority

David Flint

Toronto

OXFORD UNIVERSITY PRESS

1971

ISBN 0—19—540184—0

© Oxford University Press (Canadian Branch) 1971

1 2 3 4 5 6 — 6 5 4 3 2 1

Printed in Canada by John Deyell Limited

Contents

Illustrations

Preface

In his heyday William Lyon Mackenzie (1795-1861) was a fiery young Scot who possessed many of the characteristics of a successful political agitator. He had boundless nervous energy, an eloquent pen, a persuasive tongue, and a burning ambition to seek out injustice wherever he saw or imagined it.

From 1824 to 1837 Mackenzie devoted himself to the interests of isolated and poverty-stricken farmers and labourers. His newspaper, the *Colonial Advocate,* was at first designed to raise his readers from the intellectual deprivations of pioneer life to some knowledge of practical politics and economics and liberal trends throughout the world. It soon revealed a fervent desire to stir the province out of its apathy and to achieve for the pioneer settlers, with whom he readily identified himself, a voice in government and satisfaction for their many grievances.

Mackenzie's desire to introduce changes in the society he lived in brought him into open conflict with leading members of the government, most of whom were Tories—a name given to those who were conservative in politics and firm believers in the interdependence of Church and State. While serving the colony intelligently and honestly according to their beliefs, they saw themselves first and foremost as subjects of the Crown whose duty it was to conserve the political and economic values of eighteenth-century Britain. They were deeply opposed to democracy, which could all too easily give rise to republicanism, a form of government that in their view was "contrary to the universal order of nature, from the Divinity downwards to the communities of the meanest insects".

In attacking such things as patronage, which was rampant among government officials, Mackenzie energetically and courageously stood up to judges, governors, and politicians. In the course of frequent assaults and rebuffs he turned into a popular hero. This popularity, earned in part from journalism that often descended to muckraking and demagoguery, made him loathed by those who governed. They sought to punish Mackenzie and several times expelled him from the House of Assembly.

It was not in Mackenzie's nature to take opposition calmly and reasonably. While seeming to thrive on it, he became increasingly irrational in his behaviour—erratic, disorganized, and essentially destructive. These qualities accounted for his journalistic invective and for his wild behaviour during the abortive uprising against British rule in Upper Canada that we call the Rebellion of 1837. Mackenzie exploited the people's loyalty in organizing them to take up arms, but what he initiated he could not direct: he was a failure as a leader of men. The show of force provided by some 750 rural supporters erupted in two inglorious shooting matches. After the second the insurgents were easily dispersed by the militia— which was made up of other country people who had somewhat better leadership.

The skirmishes in Upper Canada and the more serious disturbances in Lower Canada did not directly cure any of the provinces' ills, but they did lead the British government to send Lord Durham to Canada on a mission of investigation. His *Report* helped to bring about the union of the two provinces in 1841. Responsible government—by which the representative of the Crown acts on the advice of a ministry that commands a majority in the House—came in 1849, when Britain resolved to loosen the ties of these burdensome colonies. The idea that Upper Canada should be granted a provincial ministry that would be removed if it was defeated in the House of Assembly had first been put forward by Dr William Warren Baldwin in 1828 and was developed by Robert Baldwin in 1836.

Perhaps because historians before and after the turn of the century glorified or glossed over his role in Canadian history, Mackenzie used to be thought of as a noble idealist, a public-spirited rebel against reactionary authority, and a prophetic exponent of responsible government. The brief account of his life that follows portrays a much less romantic and praiseworthy figure.

Mackenzie was not a political theorist and had no plan. In writing about the need for a representative system of government he was very vague. He was a gadfly whose main concern was to attack entrenched power in the interests of the people: it did not matter (or was not clear) to him that he did this inconsistently. His grab-bag of suggestions for change—not all of them progressive—made him a radical in the context of the times he lived in. But from a modern point of view his ideals of cheap government, low taxes, and the non-intervention of government in society make him rather conservative and even "right wing". The events he brought about in 1837 damaged the economy, caused many "useful and respectable citizens" to emigrate, and led shortly afterwards to American raids on Canada and tension between

Britain and the United States. The extreme Tory view of society became discredited in time, but the rebellion also laid to rest the extreme radicals. After the union of 1841 government was controlled by moderates—Reformers *and* Conservatives.

Though William Lyon Mackenzie did not accomplish anything positive, his career remains the liveliest and most engrossing phenomenon of the turbulent 1820s and 1830s in what is now called Ontario. We are so little accustomed to rebels and rebellions in Canada that, as we follow the wayward course of Upper Canadian history, we easily become fascinated by Mackenzie's maddening (and slightly mad) personality and by the strange mixture of the admirable and the scurrilous in his journalistic outpourings, of the idealistic and the destructive in his actions. For a short period in Canadian history and in a relatively small region, these things once loomed very large.

1

Rebel Against Authority

The story of William Lyon Mackenzie begins in Scotland. He was born in Springfield, a suburb of Dundee, in the late winter of 1795—the only child of Elizabeth and Daniel Mackenzie. The parents were noted in the community for the contrast they presented: Daniel Mackenzie, a weaver by trade, was twenty-eight when his son was born; Elizabeth was forty-five. Daniel was quick, eager, fond of fun and dancing, and had the reputation of being a philanderer. (There were those who suspected that marriage hadn't tamed him.) Elizabeth was standoffish and severe.

A Mackenzie who married a Mackenzie, Elizabeth had a sense of family pride that was "enough for a whole Scottish clan", in the words of her son many years later. When she was widowed only twenty-eight days after her son was born, she determined to raise the boy on her own, although there were relatives who could have helped. One of Mackenzie's earliest and most painful memories was of the humiliation his mother faced in trying to keep them alive during the famine of 1800-1:

I lay in bed one morning during the grievous famine . . . while my poor mother took from our large [chest] . . . the handsome plaid of the tartan of our clan, which in early life her own hands had spun, and went and sold it for a trifle to obtain for us a little coarse barley meal whereof to make our scanty breakfast.

She was later forced to sell a "hitherto carefully preserved priest-grey coat" that had belonged to Daniel—a memento of their short marriage.

Much of the motivating force behind Elizabeth Mackenzie was a dedication to Calvinist principles of hard work and independence, prayer and Bible-reading. She saw to it that her only child knew the psalms, the Bible, and the Westminster Catechism. Although in adult life he was never deeply committed to the Presbyterian Church of his youth, Mackenzie's early training never left him. He would often drag from his encyclopaedic mind miscellaneous religious verses to support his ideals and beliefs. In the midst of controversy he often convinced himself of the correctness of his stand by quoting from Holy Scripture.

Mackenzie's early education showed him to be above average in intelligence and quick at arithmetic; he was usually at the head of his class. According to his son-in-law and first biographer, Charles Lindsey, he was brash, and hostile to authority. In class Little Willie (as he was called) tied knots in the hair of girls in front of him, chalked their backs, or pinned labels on them while helping them with sums and grammar. Teachers who beat him would receive a challenging smirk. Once he was caught strutting around the classroom impersonating the teacher; he was whipped "until his face became spotted over and the bigger boys began hissing and shouting at the master". The school he attended in Dundee had at one time been a Roman Catholic chapel, and the master attempted to isolate young Mackenzie by seating him up on the "holy water" basin to be scorned and derided. Willie basked in the attention he received.

At the age of ten he rebelled against his mother and ran away from home. A castle in the Grampian Hills near Dundee attracted him and he was able to persuade a few of his companions to go with him and attempt a hermit's way of life. After several days of starvation, however, and living in fear of evil spirits and fairies, they headed for home and a joyful family reunion, which was followed no doubt by firm whacks of the rod. The boy's dreams of a blissful life away from lessons and authority did not abate and thereafter he spent much of his spare time down at the Dundee harbour, gazing longingly at the ships in the Firth of Tay and their captains who had sailed in from the North Sea. The excitement and talk of the waterfront stirred in his imagination dreams of adventures at sea. His daydreaming came to an abrupt end, however, when he impulsively dove into the Tay to retrieve some marbles: scarcely able to swim, he was dragged out half-drowned.

Willie became enraptured by books and began to read avidly; his thirst for knowledge was unquenchable. Between 1806 and 1819, when he was twenty-four, he had amassed notes on and stored in his mind the contents of 957 books. Their titles embraced theology, history, science, agriculture, education, poetry, drama, and fiction. In later life he was never at a loss to call upon famous authors to back up his opinions.

In his early teens Mackenzie left school to work as a clerk in a Dundee merchandising firm. His thirst for knowledge did not leave him and he continued his self-education with evening sessions in the library and newsroom of the Dundee *Advertiser* and by active membership in the Scientific and Literary Society. At seventeen Mackenzie was by his own admission "reckless, wild, a confirmed gambler, and some-

what dissipated (more so perhaps than I would like to own)".
He later credited the Society with improving his character.

*Had no such society existed, [I] might perhaps have been
induced oftener to exchange [my] labours at the desk of
[my] master's counting-room for the deceitful gratification
offered in the tavern or gambling house.*

But reformation was still a few restless years away.

At the age of nineteen Mackenzie borrowed capital and
ventured into business for himself. He opened a general store
and circulating library, which lasted about three years before
it went bankrupt. He had become addicted to gambling, and
only with a dedicated effort of will, supported by his
mother's stern training in Calvinism, was he able, at the age
of twenty-one, to give up the visions of quick riches and
grandeur that gaming fed. "I paused, threw down cards and
dice for ever, and became temperate." In May 1817 Mackenzie left home for greener pastures in the south of England
and for the next two and a half years drifted from job to job.
In November and December 1819 he was in France.

A mysterious chapter of Mackenzie's life was written during these years in the Old World. He fathered a son, James.
No information was left by Mackenzie to reveal the mother's
identity, and to the grandmother, Elizabeth, fell the task of
raising the boy until her son settled down and assumed the
responsibilities he had brought upon himself. For his part,
Mackenzie was anxious to leave home and rid himself of his
past. He was determined to reform, to rescue his mother
from poverty, and to pay all his debts.* He gladly accepted
the suggestion of a friend in the Scientific Society, Edward
Lesslie, that he emigrate to Canada. (Lesslie himself and his

---

* These debts, amounting to about £70, were paid when Mackenzie visited Scotland
in 1833.

six sons were planning to emigrate.) In April 1820 he set out on board the ship *Psyche*.

He was now a full-grown man. Though slight of build and, at 5 feet 6 inches, short by today's standards, his physical appearance immediately attracted attention. Charles Lindsey describes Mackenzie's massive head: "high and broad in the frontal region and well rounded . . . too large for the slight wiry frame it surmounted." Though barely twenty-five, he was completely bald. He had lost his blond hair during a fever and replaced it with a flaming red wig that he used to heighten a fit of rage or an outburst of joy by casting it on the floor or tossing it in the air as the occasion demanded. Mackenzie's formidable countenance was accentuated by his restless deep-set blue eyes and bushy brows. When he was confident his piercing eyes seemed to penetrate his adversary; when he was unsure of his position they would wander to avoid confrontation.

Soon after landing at Quebec City, Mackenzie left for Montreal, where he was able to find summer employment with the Lachine Canal Company as a chain-bearer on a survey crew. His priggish side is revealed in an incident of this period described by Samuel Thompson in *Reminiscences of a Canadian Pioneer*. The members of the surveying party sat down on a grassy bank to eat their dinner, as they always did at noon. After half an hour had passed they were getting ready for a smoke when the new chain-bearer suddenly jumped up and said: "Now, boys, time for work! We mustn't waste government money." The company decided they could do without him—exactly why is not known, though it may be that his personality rubbed everybody, men *and* management, the wrong way. In the late summer Mackenzie headed for the frontier town of York in Upper Canada.

To Mackenzie and all those who made their way west from the more civilized world of Lower Canada, York—commonly called "Muddy Little York"—was a poor excuse for a town. In the early 1820s the first sight to greet the immigrant as he stepped off the boat was several hundred shabby unpainted frame structures spread out along the shore. Homes and shops were scattered from the Don River in the east almost as far as Fort York near the Humber River in the west. Pressing tightly against the back of the community, around present-day Queen Street, was a primeval pine and hardwood forest. East of the town, marshes and swamps were clearly visible. Citizens worried about the effect of the stagnant waters on their health. "He who first fixed upon this spot as the site of the capital of Upper Canada," wrote Edward Talbot, a visitor to York in 1819, "whatever predilection he may have had for the roaring of frogs or for the effluvia arising from stagnant waters and putrid vegetables, can certainly have no very great regard for preserving the lives of his Majesty's subjects."

The most fashionable and the newest section of town was in the west. It was away from the marshes and boasted the town's first brick residences. The east end, on the other hand, was gaining a reputation for being the wrong place to live. Here were the taverns and brothels and the lower-class Irish immigrants whom the more affluent people of York considered crude. The youngsters of the area carried on a continuous and serious rivalry with their counterparts on the west side. John Carroll's reminiscences about his early life in this shabby district of York give vivid details of the children's wars in which he took part.

Jarvis Street was the boundary between their respective dominions. . . . They met on a common near the dividing line between the towns. . . . At first they were drawn up in two bodies confronting each other; still they seemed to hesitate to encounter the danger and responsibility of actual conflict. . . . Action was precipitated by some New Town boy shying a pebble which struck the Old Town commander on the top of his head. His followers rushed . . . to avenge the insult and . . . missiles of all kinds flew about in a manner dangerous to all. Both sides had provided themselves with ammunition in the shape of small stones.

The straightest street, and also the main east-west thoroughfare, was King Street, which even in its early days had speed restrictions. No person was to "gallop, or ride or drive a horse or horses at an unreasonable rate in the streets of the town or on the bank or on the beach in front of the same". Speeding was a problem mainly in the winter, when the roads were frozen and snow-covered. Horse-drawn sleighs were a menace. Francis Collins, the editor of the *Canadian Freeman,* wrote: "A poor decrepit old Scotchman named Sandy Mc-Dougall was trampled down by . . . a two-horse sleigh while carrying a bucket of water across the main street of York, and his leg is so lacerated that it is feared amputation will be necessary in order to save his life."

Walking through town a newcomer might easily pass well-dressed government officials in tailored attire or meet rustic settlers clothed in homespun or deerskin garments. Indians, who came into town to barter their crafts, salmon, or furs for flour, sugar, and tea, were a common sight. After the War of 1812 a number of blacks had left the British army and remained in town; they were being joined by freed or escaped slaves from the United States.

Settlers and farmers would come to York to take their grain to the Eastwood and Skinner gristmill on the Don River and shop, visit, and sightsee. Flour was bartered for manufactured goods and staples or, if barley or hops had been grown, farmers would bring their harvest to the Messrs Stoyell and Co. or to the John Farr brewery for a cash return. A visit to the blacksmith shop to have implements repaired or to purchase hand-forged tools was another certain errand. At the general stores and more specialized merchant shops, of which there were about fifteen, a few dollars or some farm produce would buy tea, tobacco, or a luxury like dried imported fruit or sugar.

York offered the hospitality of many inns and boarding-houses. Inns like Frank's Hotel provided not only a meeting place for town events but a ballroom and centre for travelling shows, concerts, and plays. Taverns in the east end of town were handy to the market area of Jarvis, King, Church, and Front Streets and convenient also to the steamboat wharf at the foot of Church Street. Men needed little encouragement to spend their time and money in taverns because whisky was cheap—about 25 cents a gallon.

The king's representative, Lieutenant-Governor Peregrine Maitland, was, by his wealth and ostentatious living, the most conspicuous figure in town. He was a stiff and proper military man who had served in numerous campaigns, including the Battle of Waterloo. His wife was the daughter of the Duke of Richmond, the Governor-in-Chief of British North America (to whom Maitland owed his Upper Canada appointment). Between 1818 and 1828 the social life of York and indeed the whole province revolved around Lady Sarah—much to her pleasure.

Maitland was dedicated to the economic and political advancement of the province, but his effectiveness as an administrator was limited by his aristocratic aloofness from the people. He did not govern by himself, for the British-controlled system of government allowed for the appointment of Executive and Legislative Councils. The Lieutenant-Governor personally chose the members of both. Executive Councillors advised him at his pleasure, while the Legislative Councillors acted as a conservative brake on the popularly elected House of Assembly. By 1824 most of the Executive Councillors sat in the Legislative Council as well, and it can be safely said that these few men exerted the most influence on the Lieutenant-Governor, who ran the province for the British government. All laws could of course be vetoed in Britain.

The House of Assembly—which usually met for only three months a year, from January to March—gave the appearance of popular government and appeased the North American desire for local autonomy. It was made up of members who were elected by property holders of the province for a maximum term of four years. In the minds of the governing authorities and many others, the Assemblymen were crude and ignorant—a nuisance to be avoided as much as possible. Mrs Mary O'Brien recalled in her journal that she was "amused by the parties at the inn, some with the appearance of Gentlemen, others that of greasy farmers strangely mingled together, as it seemed, by politics . . . it seemed that they were all somehow connected with the *house.*" Even Mackenzie, who became a strong supporter of the Assembly, railed at the members' lack of education. "We want more legislators who are able to sign their own names and write three words following each other without misspelling, and we must allow them to get an education somewhere."

Many people felt that the Lieutenant-Governor was overly influenced by the Reverend Dr John Strachan, a Church of England missionary and schoolmaster of the only established grammar or secondary school in York. His pastoral charge was the first and, until 1818, the only church in town. Strachan was an ambitious Scot of humble birth who had been in the province since 1800 and had worked himself into a powerful position in public life, which was greatly strengthened by his leadership of the loyalist British community in York during the War of 1812.

Strachan and Maitland were close friends and shared high ideals of Church and State. Certainly it was an advantageous friendship for Strachan, because he was able to pursue his projects with official approval. By the early 1820s education and politics had been brought under the influence of the Church of England, and for this Strachan was largely responsible. Maitland approved, for he agreed with Strachan that British loyalty and traditions could best be maintained in the province through the influence of the English Church.

Everyone had strong feelings one way or another about Strachan, but even those who, like Mackenzie, disagreed with him had to admit to a certain respect for his indomitable spirit and intangible hold on people. There was hardly a prominent person in the province who hadn't come to feel a debt of gratitude to him for his diligence and excellence as a teacher and leader of men. Many government figures had learned self-discipline and leadership under the stern tutelage of Strachan the schoolmaster. Most notable of the "Strachan boys" was John Beverley Robinson, son of a Loyalist and, since 1818 when he was only twenty-seven, Attorney-General of Upper Canada. Like his mentor, Robinson was demonstrably anti-American and pro-British.

There were other educated people in the community who had established themselves as early settlers, merchants, and important government office-holders. The Loyalist Jarvis family had come from the United States via New Brunswick.

Its most prominent members were William Botsford Jarvis, who became sheriff of the district in 1827; Stephen, the registrar and later usher in the Assembly; and Samuel Peters Jarvis, a young lawyer. Other families that had an influence on the life of York were the Boulton brothers, D'Arcy and Henry John; Christopher Hagerman; J.B. and J.S. Macaulay; and the Ridouts—George, Joseph, Samuel Smith, and Thomas. These families and their supporters, who dominated the Councils, became known as the Tories—a name that indicated their conservative Britishness rather than allegiance to a political party. They were British in background, monarchical and anti-American in politics—characteristics shared by the majority of York citizens.

There was also in York a small but vocal group of liberal and reform-minded men who, while ever loyal to the British king, voiced their opinions on the need for democratic changes in the manner of governing. Prominent among them were the Baldwins—William Warren, who was born in Ireland, and his son Robert; Jesse Ketchum, a wealthy and philanthropic tanner of American birth; and John Rolph, an English lawyer. They were not asked to sit on the Councils and might not have joined if they had been invited, for they were very critical of the extent to which Upper Canada was governed without reference to the popularly elected Assembly and would not have wanted to strengthen the power of the appointed Councils by their presence. Though their ideas were expressed in the Assembly, they were ignored elsewhere, especially by those who made most of the laws.

Outsiders considered York's petty politics very insignificant. Britain, though it had divided Upper and Lower Canada to accommodate the large French population, still looked upon the two Canadas as one administrative area: the Governor resided in the larger, wealthier, and older lower province, where customs duties were collected and shared with the western province. The only revenue Upper Canada could rely on came from Britain, and it was used to pay the salaries of government officials.

Upper Canada was an almost forgotten province. In 1820 its capital, York, was small and difficult to reach, for roads were impassable except in the wintertime. When weather permitted most mail, manufactured goods, and travellers arrived by boat—after a long and exhausting trip up the St Lawrence River and across Lake Ontario. The journey from Montreal usually took twelve days by Durham boat—a flat-bottomed barge 80 to 90 feet long, with a slip keel, round bow, square stern, and a mast. It was sailed, rowed, or poled along the river or lake by a crew of eight. Travelling upriver against the current was arduous, and at times passengers were compelled to jump into the water to help push. There were no sleeping or sanitary arrangements, nor was there any shelter from the sun or rain. Sudden squalls or storms on Lake Ontario could send ships to the bottom. Trade was slow and the mail erratic.

Upper Canada's wealth lay primarily in her vast tracts of fertile land still covered by dense virgin forest. People were needed to settle and clear the land, plant crops, and export the harvest back to Europe. After 1800 a large inflow of American settlers had been encouraged, but the War of 1812 brought this immigration to an end. The Napoleonic Wars had prevented large-scale emigration from Britain, and it was not until 1816 that a trickle of adventurers began arriving on the shores of Lake Ontario. Between 1814 and 1820 the population of York doubled to 1,250 and British immigration to Upper Canada increased steadily throughout the twenties. The Irish brought their fraternal quarrels with them, and every year on July 12 there was a riot in the streets of York between the Roman Catholic men of St Patrick and the Protestant Orangemen who were celebrating their delivery from Papist authority by King Billy—William of Orange.

But though people were starting to arrive, the economic situation remained static. Export trade was almost non-existent. The tanneries, sawmills, and breweries of York and its hinterland sold directly to the consumer and confined themselves to local trade. The farmers did produce a little wheat, flour, and potash that could be exported, and when the frozen roads would allow it they sold their goods to the York merchants, who stored them for export by boat in the spring. But there was no guarantee of the price British importers would pay, and whenever a York merchant paid a Canadian farmer for exportable produce, he took a chance. Few were willing to gamble and the whole community suffered from lack of cash; it had to rely mostly on barter.

When William Lyon Mackenzie arrived in York in 1820 he opened a drug and bookselling shop with John Lesslie, near King and Yonge Streets. It was arranged with books on the right and drugs on the left. Soon another shop—known as "Mackenzie and Lesslie, Druggists, and Dealers in Hardware, Cutlery, Jewelry, Toys, Carpenter's Tools, Nails, Groceries, Confections, Dye-Stuffs, Paints &c., at the Circulating Library"—was opened in Dundas, fifty miles to the west. As settlers began moving into the region beyond the Niagara Escarpment, Dundas became an important trade centre in competition with York. Business prospered and Mackenzie decided to buy out John Lesslie in March 1823. The purchase, which included the stock, cost Mackenzie over £686.*

* There were three currencies in local use: the dollar, the pound sterling, and the Halifax pound.

Six months later he sold out, moved to Queenston near Niagara Falls, and there opened a general store.

Mackenzie's stay in Upper Canada had not been devoted entirely to business. In 1822 his mother emigrated with his son James, and the twenty-seven-year-old Mackenzie went to Montreal to meet them. They were accompanied by a gentle Scottish girl, Isabel Baxter, a former schoolmate of Mackenzie's. If Elizabeth Mackenzie picked Isabel as a suitable wife for her son she showed a remarkable instinct, for within three weeks of her arrival, on July 1, they were married.

The Queenston store thrived: after three years in the Canadas and three different jobs Mackenzie was on his way to business success. He was elected to the school board and attended freemason meetings. He began to size up the political and social situation and very soon resolved to mend the faults he saw in Upper Canadian society. Throughout the winter of 1823 and the spring of 1824 he planned and made arrangements to start the newspaper that became the *Colonial Advocate*. The first issue was published on May 18, 1824. Eight hundred copies were printed and Mackenzie mailed them out at his own expense to selected potential subscribers, not only in Upper Canada but in Great Britain and the United States.

The first few issues of this "Journal of Agriculture, Manufactures and Commerce", as it was subtitled, were smaller than the usual newspaper and were folded into a booklet measuring 14 by 6 inches. They were printed in the United States, both as an economy measure and to attract an American following, for news items and gossip from both countries were featured. Like most newspapers of the day in the Canadas, the *Colonial Advocate* was a one-man effort. Mackenzie wrote, edited, and mailed it himself, and the articles and fillers it contained reflected his own point of view. Very often he compared American and Canadian economic policies and government systems; perhaps inevitably, because of the prosperity of the United States, he appeared to favour the American. In the earliest issues he stated that "from personal knowledge of both countries" he knew that "Canada is much worse off for religious instruction than the United States", and that Canada "has so long languished in a state of comparative stupor and inactivity whilst our more enterprising neighbours are laughing us to scorn". Statements such as these did not endear him to the York establishment, who were trying to enforce a strict anti-American, pro-British feeling in the province. Chief Justice Powell and the government paper, the *Upper Canada Gazette*, criticized Mackenzie's opinions and dismissed the *Colonial Advocate* as an American paper.

By July the paper's format had changed to the common newspaper sheet of five long columns. Letters, news, advertisements, advice, and personals were inserted at random in tiny print. It was now printed in Queenston. In the edition of July 1 Mackenzie hit out at Powell and the Tory criticisms that were aimed at discrediting him because earlier *Advocate*s had been printed in the United States.

The first 12 numbers of the Advocate *are printed by contract 400 yards east of the Niagara River. Fault is found with this by the Justice. We plead in justification the example of a Legislative Councillor, 2 Colonels, 4 M.P.s, a few dozen merchants, and five Canal Commissioners of Upper Canada who all crossed over to the cheapest market for their advertisements. . . . The example of the Justice himself, who, though he sent to London for his Annual Register types, went to Yankee town for the octavo paper on which that publication is to be printed; nay more, who prints in York our laws and Gazettes in brown paper of America, with types of America, and not seldom with the aid of American journeymen to boot . . . in short, as from necessity our teas etc. come from the United States, so also does the profit, interest and advantage of all our public undertakings revert to, and increase the wealth, commerce, and manufacturing of the said States.*

Mackenzie proceeded to discuss other weaknesses in the provincial administration. Ignoring the geographic disadvantages of Upper Canada, the lack of capital, and the meagre population, he blamed the economic woes solely on the government leaders. They were not interested in the citizens' welfare, only in their own. As for Lieutenant-Governor Maitland, "For the present," wrote Mackenzie on May 18, "we cannot remember anything he has done of a public nature worth recording . . . unless that he . . . recommended a further tax on whisky. . . . What road has he made? What Canal has begun in his time? Of what agricultural society is he the patron, president or benefactor?"

Mackenzie was not only taking an interest in government; his early writings also show a growing social conscience. He complained bitterly whenever Canadian authorities allowed an escaped slave to be turned over to the Americans.

One day last summer a poor black girl, who had escaped from the whip-lash to this side [of] the water, was seized on a Sunday near Queenston in broad daylight, between eleven and noon, by two hired scoundrels who hauled and pulled her through that village; she screaming and crying in the most piteous and heartrending manner and her ruffian cream-coloured tormentors laughing at her distress and amusing the villagers with the cock-and-bull story that she had stolen five hundred dollars . . . .

A few more ads began to appear in the *Advocate* ("Honey and Beeswax for Sale", "Imported Nails and Coffee Newly Arrived"). Mr Richard Thompson and Co. of Waterloo (near Fort Erie) advertised in large type his impressive selection of wares: groceries, spices, liquors, glass, crockery, hardware, iron and steel, hosiery, haberdashery, dry goods, dye stuffs, oils and paints, hollowware, medicines, shoemaker's articles, blacksmith tools, and the *Almanack* for 1825. In each issue there was an item about the theft of someone's horse or oxen with the reward posted, or about women wanted for household help. There were birth notices (quintuplets were born and died in Maryland) and obituaries, sometimes with comment (did Colonel Nichol *really die accidentally*?); and publicity was given to a new medical school in St Thomas and to the monument being erected in Queenston in memory of General Brock.

Mackenzie responded to the growing interest in his paper by indulging his fondness for giving advice and instruction on a wide variety of subjects. "Spectacles are always preferable [to a monocle] because both eyes, by being kept in action, are kept in health," he declared; and, "no man ever prospered in this world without the consent and co-operation of his wife."

Tobacco is a sedative, emetic, diuretic, cathartic and errhine, whether it be taken into the stomach or externally applied . . . from its narcotic powers, the smoking or chewing tobacco has been found useful in allaying the pain of toothache and in some instances in shortening and rendering more supportable the paroxysms of spasmodic asthma.

And in August there was a long article on manure.

The substances which make excellent manure are much more numerous than seems to be generally supposed by farmers. Among many others are the following: putrified fish, bones, woollen rags, fish, bacteria, soap suds, urine of all animals . . . dung of all kinds, scrapings of door yards and streets, rubbish of old houses, lime, plaster of paris, mud from ponds, rivers, swamps, and the sea, shells, turfs, ashes, earth that has been long under cover, weeds that grow in gardens . . . refuse, hay . . . .

The list goes on, ending with instructions for making a compost. Mackenzie was proud to be of help to farmers. To widen their knowledge he included in his newspaper long articles about international trade and political trends. "We believe this *Advocate* to be as rare a curiosity as any newspaper that was ever printed in the world," he boasted, giving thanks for his increased patronage.

Gradually political invective took over the *Colonial Advocate* and it became something more than a compendium of advice and miscellaneous information. Mackenzie took his politics seriously. When the elections for Assembly seats were held in the summer of 1824, he waged an all-out campaign against the incumbents. He intended to set before the politically innocent farmers the blatant truth about their government. "Many members of our Legislature get less useful the longer they are kept in parliament," he wrote dryly. "The disinterested ambassador extraordinary and minister plenipotentiary of Upper Canada, John Beverley Robinson Esquire" —who at this time described Mackenzie in a letter as "a conceited red-haired fellow with an apron"—rated four-and-a-half columns of venom.

You have been alternately the footstool and pincushion of power—you have retained that fawning cringing manner which is to the acute discerner the most sure sign of political dependence and degradation.

And he went on to inveigh against S.P. Jarvis, Judge H.J. Boulton, and the Reverend John Strachan (though he ran for no office). Mackenzie begged the farmers to sit up, take notice, and exercise their franchise independently.

If we should see a Sherwood from Prescott, a Hagerman from Kingston, and an Ambassador Robinson from York again elevated by yourselves as your representatives, we should almost despair of your privileges. But from you we hope better things.

A few reform-minded men from the eastern counties were elected to the Assembly, but for the most part the House remained the same. Not only had Mackenzie failed to remove the pro-government men, but now they began to retaliate. To the amazement of the censorious editor and the people of Queenston, one day in early July Colonel Clark, a prominent local figure and a Legislative Councillor, ordered stonemasons to tear down the work they had done on the Brock monument and remove the first-edition copy of the *Colonial Advocate* from the cornerstone.

By the autumn of 1824 Mackenzie had decided that he was too far from the centre of political action. After the November 18 edition of the *Colonial Advocate* was issued he packed up his family, possessions, and business and moved to York.

2

Journalist and Politician

When Mackenzie and his family arrived in the capital of Upper Canada in 1824 they moved into a house on Palace (now Front) Street, southeast of the English church and overlooking the bay. The printing business, newspaper office, and bookstore were installed on the ground floor, while the Mackenzies, as was the common practice of most York merchants and businessmen, lived in a flat upstairs.

York was much larger and somewhat different than when Mackenzie left it four years earlier. Government surveyors, land agents, and members of the Executive Council who were responsible for land policies had been trying for years to get people to bolster the lagging economy. Now Upper Canada's fertile countryside was finally attracting immigrants. Six hundred people had come and stayed, and many more than twice that number had passed through on their way to farms in the surrounding countryside. Most were from the British Isles. Immigrant families from Scotland and Ireland travelled together in groups and often settled on adjacent land, whereas English families usually came separately and scattered over the province.

The merchants in town were kept busy. From their homes and little shops that opened onto York's crooked, muddy streets they sold oxen, harnesses, wagons, axes, seed corn, kettles, and all the myriad essentials for homesteading. Hotels and taverns were booming, and auctioneers prospered.

The town was administered by magistrates, who were usually local merchants and professional men appointed by the Lieutenant-Governor.* They left the actual policing of the town to appointed constables, whose capability and authority were usually tenuous. Nevertheless order was maintained—in the old-fashioned British way: swift and severe punishment for any local or transient who caused trouble. Mackenzie reported in his paper that two black men in their thirties, Thomas Walden and George Scroggin, were committed to jail upon the oath of John Boels of Markham and charged with stealing two sheep. They were found guilty and sentenced to be hanged. Twenty-four-year-old John Wilson, found guilty of stealing a silver watch, was imprisoned for two months and publicly whipped with thirty-nine lashes. Women as well as men were chained into stocks on the King Street Common, to be jeered at for committing petty crimes. For stealing goods worth fifteen shillings from a York store, William Hollis was sentenced to death. He endured two years' imprisonment before the sentence was commuted.

Another kind of death—from disease—came even more swiftly, to rich and poor alike. Although vaccination was available, lack of public acceptance resulted in periodic outbreaks of smallpox. Every winter children died in epidemics of measles and scarlet fever, while "galloping consumption" (tuberculosis) was a year-round threat to everyone. Ague—a malarial fever marked by regularly recurring chills—was also

* In 1831 the magistrates were Alexander McDonell and James FitzGibbon, ex-military men; Alexander Wood and Robert Stanton, businessmen; Charles Small and D'Arcy Boulton, lawyers; and Grant Powell and Christopher Widmer, doctors.

The house Mackenzie lived and worked in on Palace (now Front) Street, at the corner of Frederick, when he moved to York in 1824. This was the property that

common around York. In 1819 Edward Talbot blamed York's location for this illness.

The situation of the town is very unhealthy, for it stands on a piece of low marshy land which is better calculated for a frog pond or beaver-meadow than for the residence of human beings. The inhabitants are on this account subject, particularly in spring and autumn, to agues and intermittent fevers; and probably five-sevenths of the people are annually afflicted with these complaints.

Talbot was no doubt partly correct, but practices common in that day, such as leaving garbage and dead animals on the frozen bay to be washed into the lake in the spring and throwing refuse from the butcher's shop into a stinking heap outside the back door, were infinitely more hazardous than frog and beaver ponds.

The Mackenzies did not escape untouched. Disease struck the family shortly after they arrived in November 1824. A little girl, named after Isabel, died of smallpox in December. Fortunately James remained healthy. Mackenzie, who wanted sons so badly, would have three more. The Mackenzies had thirteen children in all. Five died in infancy and one at thirteen years; five daughters and two sons lived to be adults.

Mackenzie spent most of 1825 trundling through the countryside trying to drum up paying customers for his newspaper. He loved to stop and visit with people, and he had a habit of gathering and passing on information, gossip, and news. More often than not he would ask questions and listen to settlers' troubles and complaints. He found that in the Kingston area the War of 1812 had not been forgotten, and indeed that the people there feared another American invasion. In the area north of York there was more concern

William Lyon Mackenzie, born at Springfield, Dundee, Forfarshire, Scotland, March 12th, 1795. Baptized on the 29th, by the Reverend Mr. Mackwen, Seceder Minister

Isabel Baxter, 2nd daughter of Peter Baxter, ... in Dundee, and of Barbara Baillie his wife, was born at Dundee, July 29th, 1802.

On Wednesday, the eighth day of April, 1829, at nine o'clock in the evening, in the town of York, Upper Canada, Isabel, wife of William L. Mackenzie, was safely delivered of a daughter.

Attested by Isabella B...

Page from the Mackenzie Family Bible. Mackenzie House.

about roads; and to the west of the Grand River, down near the Talbot settlement, there was bitterness towards domineering landlords. At the end of six months he had seen more than half the settled part of the province, an experience that made him a dedicated supporter of the interests of rural people.

During these trips Mackenzie's economic ideas began to jell and he proceeded to work out policies that would help the pioneers. Trade, or rather the lack of it, was perhaps his biggest concern, and he felt the government had not acted to meet the settlers' needs. Mackenzie had listened to the grumbling of many a farmer who had grain to sell but no easy way of getting it to market. In an age when water travel was by far the cheapest and fastest way of transporting goods, harbours and canals were of primary importance. It irritated Mackenzie to realize that natural harbour locations would not be developed because all too often waterfront properties were controlled by wealthy businessmen, some of whom lived in England. In fact he discovered that these lands were frequently political gifts from the government for favours received. He wrote in the *Colonial Advocate*:

I . . . learnt that during Colonel Burwell's parliamentary career his loyalty had got him both sides of the bank at the mouth of Otter Creek granted free by the Provincial Government—a valuable present truly. How much more correct it would have been if this spot had been laid out in lots reserved as the site of a future town; or granted only on condition that the grantee build a harbour for the protection of trade.

While journeying over long trails leading to backwood huts, or during heated discussions in the clearings, or perhaps while sharing settlers' meals of corn mush and salt pork, Mackenzie saw why the pioneers' original dreams of a glorious new beginning, great estates, and social equality were so difficult to sustain. Struggling families were isolated and lonely. They missed friends, schools, churches, and doctors, all of which were taken for granted in the old country. Life was desperately hard. Husbands were sometimes forced to leave home for months at a time to labour for a bit of cash to supplement their homestead existence, and it often seemed to the settlers that they were fighting the forest alone. New neighbours were slow to arrive because land was expensive—at least $2.50 per acre in 100-acre lots, one fourth down and the rest in annual instalments. The government had purposely set the price high to prevent speculators from accumulating too much land, but often this policy seemed to penalize the few settlers who were willing to buy. Indeed many gave up and left for the States or returned to England. Others, like Thomas Burger, decided to make the best of the situation.

In the *Colonial Advocate* Mackenzie recorded a conversation with Burger, who complained that his investment in 100 acres was a swindle because others could not afford to settle close by and make possible such amenities as roads, a school, a church, and a store. "If", said Burger, "I had known that the township was not to be settled, I would have purchased elsewhere, but now I and my family are here we must do as well as we can." Mackenzie's comment was: "It would surely be a wise[r] policy to sell these lands cheaply, [and] settle them ... than to sell a few lots and induce families to establish themselves in a permanent desert."

Despite the isolation of the farms, a comradeship developed between country folk that was never possible in the society-conscious towns. Any neighbour, newcomer, or lost traveller who happened to pass a homestead by day or night was gladly accepted as a friend, asked to dinner, and urged to share news and opinions. Farm people welcomed any excuse to get together, and whenever possible they arranged church services, barn raisings, quilting bees, political meetings, and maple-sugar feasts. On these special occasions they met, courted, competed, exchanged tales, and cheered each other's spirits. But all too many discovered that the easiest way to forget loneliness, insecurity, and the day-in, day-out struggle to wrest a living from the land was to drown themselves in liquor. It was a moderate drinker who did not have more than four glasses a day. Imported wine and spirits were available for the wealthy. The rest drank homemade gut-rot whisky, which was abundantly provided at every gathering. Because of its poor quality—it was often made of decaying potatoes, hemlock, pumpkins, and black mouldy rye—it caused more problems than it cured, including liver disease and speedy alcoholism, to say nothing of fights, accidents and various kinds of crime.

The settlers blamed the government or townsfolk (the two were becoming synonymous) for many of their troubles, and it was easy to see why. No matter how hard the farmers worked, they seemed to make little progress, while the people in town—the merchants, government officers, lawyers and tradesmen—became more and more prosperous. They had capital to invest and were able to speculate in real estate and help finance canals and commercial enterprises. Also, their influence in government circles brought them a bank charter and a guarantee of its monopoly in the province. The Bank of Upper Canada was very necessary to provincial trade and commerce because it provided capital (though not without discrimination), but in the eyes of the farmers, many of whom did not understand banking or commerce, it stood as a monument to the liaison between wealthy townsmen and government. Mackenzie glorified the settlers. "On you alone, Farmers, does Canada rely," he proclaimed. "You are the only true nobility that this country can boast of."

In spite of his inflammatory criticisms of the town establishment and its dominant role in the provincial government, Mackenzie was aware that the merchants and officials of York were not solely responsible for Upper Canada's economic ills, that ultimately Britain controlled the destiny of the province. He boldly suggested that Britain could improve her past policies. He presented a great international scheme: a special colonial legislature in England with elected representatives from all the overseas colonies, not just from Upper and Lower Canada. Mackenzie believed that a world-wide legislative body would be more immune to corruption than provincial assemblies, and that it could persuade Great Britain to stop using Upper Canada as a dumping ground for her manufactured products and give the Canadian industries a chance. He also felt that Britain should not give away any more Canadian land to English political favourites because they cared nothing for the future of the province and were content to be absentee landlords or, worse still, to leave the land idle. Some of these ideas were sound, but Mackenzie vastly underestimated the time and co-operation that were necessary to implement any one of them.

Through the *Colonial Advocate* he set about to encourage Canadians to press demands for justice in the British parliament. Throughout the spring of 1825 he frantically published the paper between various trips to the countryside, but despite his valiant efforts to drum up interest in both his paper and its suggestions for reform, the people were apathetic and the *Colonial Advocate* remained a losing proposition. Faced with a debt of £1,400 in overdue accounts,

Mackenzie hired a collector who, after an eleven-week tour covering 1,200 miles, rounded up only £42 13s 10d and claimed £15 of that amount for personal expenses. It would appear that the settlers were glad to receive the *Advocate* but not so anxious to pay for it. Mackenzie distributed 830 copies of each issue, but he had only 330 paid subscriptions.

Postage was another financial drain and gave rise to a further complaint. British postal rates were high and had to be paid in advance every three months. In contrast to the American policy of putting as much political and cultural reading material as possible into the hands of settlers, the British attitude that reading was a privilege of the upper classes and publishing the pastime of wealthy men was considered by Mackenzie to be downright ridiculous. He pointed out that Britain would cause an influx of American literature and the development of an American bias by charging prohibitive postal rates, thereby destroying Canadian publishing. "The post office is merely a monopoly retained by the government for the public good and ought to be conducted so as to be of the greatest benefit possible," he moralized. At this point he was optimistic that Britain herself would reform the system.

Worry over money, the threatened failure of his paper, and a series of illnesses made the last six months of 1825 practically unbearable for Mackenzie. The *Colonial Advocate* did not appear at all. He briefly considered moving back to Dundas. Late in the year, however, he found the means to reissue his paper. Several months later he decided to change its content and approach. In April 1826 he wrote that it would proclaim "nothing of a political or controversial character" but instead would be strictly a literary and scientific publication, which presumably would require less time and emotional strain to produce. He went on to say:

I shall be then freed from a toilsome and irksome depen-
dence, and if I lose thereby all political influence over the
minds of people, I shall gain in exchange what is to me of far
greater importance, a more extensive command of my own
time.

In reality he was lobbying for the job of King's Printer in
an attempt to salvage his business, and his pledge to stay
away from political comment was designed to attract the
government authorities to his cause. He knew that the previous Printer, Assemblyman Charles Fothergill, had been fired
for criticizing the government for withholding financial information about land dealings. A King's Printer must be neutral
regardless of his political responsibilities! Hence Mackenzie's
change of subject matter. He needed the money that went
with the position.

Mackenzie's ambitions were ignored, however. He began to
feel a little guilty for soliciting a cosy government job, and to
make amends he attempted to justify the patriotism of anyone who criticized the government.

A patriot . . . is a friend to his country. [He] studies the
laws and institutions of his nation, that he may improve
others . . . [he] associates only with those whose private con-
duct is in unison with their public professions. He is not a
mob hunter, nor a lecturer of the multitude; he desires rather
the secret approbation of the enlightened few than the
ephemeral popularity of the many. If he is a member of
Parliament he looks carefully into the merits of the question
and votes consistently with his conscience, whether with or
against the ministry. He is neither a place hunter nor a
sinecure hunter. He promises his constituents very little but
tries to perform a great deal.

Mackenzie complained to his readers that "the proprietor and editor is and must be a slave." Writing the paper, keeping accounts, and "dunning careless subscribers in all directions" demanded six full days' work a week, and he was required to sit up several nights to superintend the printing as well. On Sunday, "instead of being fit to attend church [and] read the scriptures", he would stay in bed or on the sofa, "as a temporary relief from the effects of incessant toil".

Since most of his readers were country people, Mackenzie took a swipe at selfish farmers who could well afford to pay him but didn't. *They* were not forced to trust in "the caprice of the multitude" as he was. The debts mounted and in May 1826 one of his creditors threatened to have him arrested unless he paid up.

While friends and foes alike awaited the financial collapse of the *Colonial Advocate,* Mackenzie kept up his frantic efforts to stay in business. Besides his regular features he often wrote controversial articles under pseudonyms and contributed "letters to the editor". He was always ready to publish writings by reformers—especially if they damned the establishment or reinforced his ideas. A popular contributor was Egerton Ryerson, a twenty-four-year-old convert from the English Church to Methodism, who signed his pieces "A Methodist Preacher". Mackenzie loved to print anything that called down John Strachan and the Church of England, and one front-page article—a review of a Strachan sermon by Ryerson—was an all-out attack on the views of this most prominent York Tory.

The mood of the *Colonial Advocate* now reflected its owner's worried state of mind; the paper often contained ill-considered, intemperate, and scandalous articles. In the issue of March 23 Mackenzie had sarcastically reported the

Reverend Dr John Strachan's departure for England.

The episcopal clergy of these colonies enjoy themselves right pleasantly, trotting and sailing backwards and forwards between the land of promotion and British America.

Then he went digging for some gossip. Strachan had fired the clerk of the local Church of England congregation, John Fenton (who was also a Methodist). Shortly thereafter Strachan made a complete about-face and rehired him. In April Mackenzie intimated in his newspaper that the reinstatement of Fenton was an attempt to hush up some conflict in Strachan's church.

Clerk of the Church—A New Era!—Mr Fenton, as it is said, having announced a forthcoming pamphlet upon the state of the York congregation, the doctor made him new advances, and he has actually been reinstated as clerk of our Episcopal Church with an additional salary.

In Strachan's absence, J.B. Macaulay wrote to Mackenzie protesting the inaccuracy of his insinuation. He signed himself "One of the Churchwardens". When he discovered that Fenton himself had written to deny the implications of the newspaper article, he asked Mackenzie not to publish but to return his own letter.

Mackenzie refused to honour Macaulay's request because the churchwarden's letter had not confined itself to the Fenton issue but cast aspersions on the editor's own character. Macaulay had written:

Such fabrications cannot answer the ends you aim at; they are only calculated to injure those you think to serve and to provoke the just indignation of your readers.

That Mackenzie took offence at such restrained criticism shows how easily he could be upset in these anxious days. He launched a personal attack against Macaulay.

Had the churchwarden confined his remarks to his fellow functionary, "the clerk", we would most readily have distributed the types of his letter yesterday, as he requested. But the tone he has seen fit to assume towards ourselves is not to be borne. There was a time when we looked upon that churchwarden *as one that would become the most open, manly, and independent of his class, but it has gone by. We prized his talents, his abilities, and his judgment far too high.* . . . *The churchwarden, who is not one of our subscribers, will find tomorrow that even to him we shall not meanly truckle, nor shall we to any man, although the blackest poverty should be, on earth, our reward.*

Macaulay made himself look foolish by engaging in a public correspondence with Mackenzie in the pages of the *Colonial Advocate*; he even went to the trouble of publishing a special pamphlet in which he questioned Mackenzie's past business dealings, mocked his ancestry, and jeered at his mother. Here was Macaulay using the journalistic tactics of name-calling that Mackenzie had made his own.

Mackenzie's response was crude and even more malicious. In the May 18 issue of the *Colonial Advocate* he reported on an imaginary gathering of six friends who had met to read and discuss "the works of J.B. Macaulay, being a common standard for stupidity in Upper Canada". They "were punctual to the old-fashioned hour of seven and after the cloth had been removed and the wine, biscuit, and tumblers duly placed before his guests, Mr Swift desired Mr Hopkins to proceed with the business of the evening." Macaulay was severely dismembered. The fictional Mr Caleb Hopkins commented on Macaulay's personal appearance, spoke of "that pitiful, mean-looking parasite", an "up-start varlet" and "a stink-pot of government", and charged him with the crime of "having begun life as a barber's apprentice". The others joined in:

Brown: "It is a wonder how so ordinary a fellow as this Macaulay got into the council, or into any situation above that of a bum bailiff."

Doctor Tod: "I can give you a reason for his nose being crooked upwards, and a good one it is. His father intended him at first for his own trade of an apothecary and kept him pounding stinking gum for hysteric pills to old women until the horrid smell of the drug actually turned his nose into a peg, whereon his grandfather might have safely hung up his fiddle."

*   *   *   *

Swift: "Is Macaulay an infidel?"

Doctor Tod: "He is the churchwarden of the Episcopalians, and how far that is from being an infidel I leave it to you to guess."

Mackenzie then turned his attention to a few other prominent York citizens, also members of the Church of England. His first target was John Beverley Robinson, whom he had attacked before in his Queenston publishing days. "Have the Robinsons anything to boast of in their Virginian descent? . . . Is it a secret in these parts that many, very many, such Virginian nobles, as the Robinsons assume themselves, were descended from mothers who came here to try their luck and were purchased by their sires with tobacco at prices according to the quality and soundness of the article?" He taunted Robinson about the fact that his widowed mother once "kept the cake and beer shop in King Street, York". Class and social background were important marks of distinction in the early 1800s and Mackenzie was anxious to let his readers know that those in charge of the province came from the same sort of "low" background that he did.

In the issue of June 8 Mackenzie revived a nine-year-old scandal involving members of two of York's most prominent families. John Ridout and Samuel Jarvis had met in the early morning of July 12, 1817 for a duel on a farm north of York.* As it was still dark outside, and raining, they and their seconds waited in a barn for daylight and for the skies to clear. Finally the young men went out and took up their positions facing each other eight yards apart. They were ordered to fire at the count of three. At the second count Ridout nervously fired at Jarvis and missed. He apologized for his mistake and asked for another weapon, but the referee decreed that, according to the duelling code, he must stand to face his opponent's fire. Ridout stood firm, was shot in the chest, carried into the barn, and left to die. In the resulting trial Chief Justice Powell found the defendant not guilty, the usual custom when the authorities were not able to head off duels before they took place. In the ensuing nine years the Ridout-Jarvis families suffered greatly as a result of the duel, but Mackenzie simply could not resist using a human-interest story to make a case against the solid upper-class community of York, whom he considered to be united against himself and all others who were poverty-stricken.

Although the older members of the community establishment might have fumed privately over Mackenzie's writings, it was the younger set that took action. Mackenzie was out of town when a group of well-dressed gentlemen banged at the *Advocate*'s office door. Both his mother and James were in the flat upstairs but they were too frightened to answer. Receiving no response, the men forced their way in and

* At present-day College and Yonge Streets.

proceeded to wreck the press and smash some type cases. Into the bay went the type to join the town's garbage, while many people—including the Auditor-General, Colonel Heward, and the Honourable William Allen—looked on.

The incident evoked sympathetic comment from another outspoken editor, Francis Collins, an Irishman who habitually opposed the government and everyone else as well. The *Canadian Freeman* declared:

In little York it seems that a man's house is his castle only while he crouches to official arrogance and licks the hand of petty tyranny—and the moment that the dignity of his nature recoils from servility, his castle is to be razed to the very ground.

Mackenzie's published list of the attackers reveals the extent to which he had united the government establishment in opposition to himself. Among others there were Charles and Raymond Bâby, sons of James Bâby, the Inspector-General. John Lyons took part; he was the private secretary to the Lieutenant-Governor. Henry, the son of Judge Sherwood, was there, as well as Charles Heward, the son of the Auditor-General. A student in the office of Solicitor-General Boulton, James King, was a conspicuous member of the gang, and so was Samuel P. Jarvis, the survivor of the duel.

Mackenzie pressed a civil suit against the men for damages, and a trial was set for October. A jury—three men from York and nine from the rural areas—was chosen to judge the case. Evidence for the plaintiff was ably given by his lawyers, Marshall Spring Bidwell and James Small. The defence was conducted by Christopher Hagerman and J.B. Macaulay. After a debate of thirty-two hours the jury decided on an award of £625 (about $2,450) to compensate the owner of the *Colonial Advocate*. (It was rumoured around town that

Mackenzie said his losses amounted to only $45.) To pay for the damages James FitzGibbon—Colonel of the Militia, Deputy Adjutant-General, and Justice of the Peace—passed around a hat to the town's upper crust, an act Francis Collins considered immoral (FitzGibbon was a public servant), especially since he thought the Lieutenant-Governor himself had made a contribution. James Bâby, of course, was approached. "There," he said sarcastically to his son Raymond as he handed over his contribution, "go and make one great fool of yourself again." Probably no rioter paid more than $10—a cheap way to end freedom of the press, in the opinion of Collins. Mackenzie professed amazement "that because a little scurrility is published in a newspaper, destruction of property is justified and a peace officer collects the money."

However, the destruction of Mackenzie's printing office was a blessing in disguise. The sudden windfall of over two thousand dollars put Mackenzie on the black side of the ledger once more, and the *Colonial Advocate* was revived. But the tensions of past controversies and struggle had taken their toll on him personally. "My health had for three or four months been in the most precarious state," he wrote, "and much sickness in my family had depressed my spirits beyond anything I had ever felt or endured before."

The health of his family improved after the favourable court judgement, but not the temper of the *Colonial Advocate*. On December 7, 1826 Mackenzie published the first issue of the paper since June. He vowed to retain its candid and independent character and in a condescending and perhaps appeasing manner declared that he would postpone reviewing the press-types persecution until a later date when he could be more objective, though over the next eight years—until the demise of the *Colonial Advocate*—he continually referred to this incident to reinforce his arguments against the ruling class.

Now that the *Colonial Advocate* was firmly re-established, Mackenzie was more confident of himself and became inexorably and more deeply drawn into the political hassels of the province. These could not easily be resolved because Britain had to intervene, or at least be consulted, on every major issue, and letters took six weeks or more to reach England and just as long to be answered. Between the revival of the *Advocate* and the Assembly elections in July 1828, three political problems commanded the attention of the watchful Mackenzie and his newspaper. The first, the most consequential to the population and the lengthiest, was the "alien question".

Before the War of 1812 Governor Simcoe had encouraged and welcomed numerous American settlers*—some were even given large land grants—but the war ended immigration from the United States. The Tory leaders of Upper Canadian society (such as Strachan and his former pupils, lawyers H.J. Boulton and John Beverley Robinson, as well as George Markland and Christopher Hagerman—all prominent government figures during the 1820s) noticed that many American settlers had only grudgingly supported Britain. In the minds of the Tories an independent Canada demanded the maintenance of a British identity, and they were determined that in the future American anti-monarchical politics and democratic institutions should be banned from Canadian territory. To this end they urged that severe restrictions be placed on the number of American immigrants.

Loyalty to England, or the lack of it, became a frantic

---

*The population of Upper Canada was approximately 90,000, of which about 75,000 were Americans or of American descent.

preoccupation of many government leaders. On at least one occasion it brought about disgraceful, and somewhat comic, results. On New Year's Eve 1825 Captain John Matthews, Assemblyman for Middlesex—broadminded, intelligent, but despised by some because of his outspoken support of Unitarianism—had gone to the Mansion House Hotel in York. He and a group of about sixteen Assemblymen had just finished a heated debate on the merits of American immigration and decided to enjoy a performance given by an American touring company at the hotel. Much liquor was consumed, and at the end of the show, when spirits were high, members of the audience shouted out requests to the band. Matthews jovially called out for "Yankee Doodle". Others had asked for "Hail Columbia" or "Rule Britannia"—probably a jest on the earlier debate. During "Yankee Doodle" there were mock patriotic cries of "Off with your hats!" and in their exuberance some Assemblymen pounded their friends on the back. When the Governor of the Canadas and commander-in-chief, Lord Dalhousie, heard of Matthews' request, he charged him with disloyalty and had his pension cut off. Many Assemblymen were furious over this inane treatment and picked a committee to investigate the hotel incident and have the Colonial Office rectify the matter if the facts so warranted.* While the committee was calling witnesses to testify, the Upper Canadian government took a stand against Americanism.

In 1826 the Naturalization (or Alien) Bill was passed by the Upper Canadian government. Based on terms set out by Lord Bathurst, the Colonial Secretary, on the advice of anti-American colonial leaders—including Sir Peregrine Maitland, who had been influenced by wartime residents of York

---

* It was not until May 8, 1828 that the *Colonial Advocate* could report that Captain Matthews' pension had been restored.

—it stated that British citizenship and its political privileges would not be granted to Americans until they had lived in the province for seven years, subscribed to oaths and declarations of loyalty to the king, and renounced their allegiance to the United States.

Most of the men of American background elected to the Assembly had not renounced allegiance to the United States, nor had they taken an oath of loyalty to the king; even now they did not feel either was necessary. The naturalization laws implied that the long-term American-born residents of Canada were disloyal and brought into question their right to sit in the Assembly. Rumours spread rapidly that the Alien Bill was an excuse to boot out of the Assembly any members who opposed the laws preventing unrestricted American immigration.

American Assemblymen, their friends, and Mackenzie's newspaper fought to change the bill. At a meeting on February 21, 1827, at Snyder's Yonge Street tavern, a select committee of several prominent Americans in York was formed; it was called the "Central Committee of the Inhabitants of Upper Canada whose rights are affected by the provisions of the Alien Bill". Jesse Ketchum was chairman and treasurer.* Mackenzie acted as secretary and was the moving spirit in promoting a petition to back complaints to the British government about the restrictions on so-called aliens. The *Colonial Advocate* of February 22 pleaded with Anglo-Americans to petition the king as quickly as possible.

---

* Others on the committee were Jordan Post, a watchmaker from Connecticut and later owner of a sawmill in Scarborough; Dr Alexander Burnside, one-time innkeeper and later founder of the Burnside Lying-in Department of the Toronto General Hospital and a benefactor of Trinity College; Dr Thomas Stoyell; and Joseph Shepherd.

To induce people to immigrate into this country... to send them into our forests to create fruitful fields out of the everlasting wilderness... ever to be cooped up and tyrannized over in Upper Canada... there to be sneered at, scoffed and mocked as the Yankee Doodle half-subjects of a mountebank ministry—forbid it, British justice! Forbid it, ye peers of England whose untarnished honour hath upheld the state... forbid it, thou great monarch who art deservedly held by us thy subjects as incapable of doing us wrong.

Although Mackenzie could be critical of Britain—particularly of her colonial trade policy—he firmly believed that the British parliamentary system guaranteed freedom, and that if the injustices of the Upper Canadian authorities could be made known to the British legislators, they would immediately intervene.

Mackenzie later claimed that there were 15,000 signatures on the petition, which had been passed around the countryside. Those who signed were not necessarily pro-American; but they knew that more settlers, regardless of nationality, were needed to open up the land. Many recent British immigrants who did not have the experience of the War of 1812 to colour their views also gave their support.

In March 1827 Assemblyman Robert Randal, a Virginian by birth and an old friend and confidant of Mackenzie's from his Queenston days, took the petition to England to convince the Colonial Office of the loyalty of Americans in Upper Canada and the need to amend the bill. The ultra-loyalist faction of the province was astounded when Lord Goderich, the Colonial Secretary, not only met with Randal in June but shortly afterwards reversed his position and disallowed the bill, making it possible for the Canadian legislature to pass a law automatically conferring citizenship on settlers who had come into the province before 1820, and requiring a seven-year waiting period only for those who had arrived after that date. The *Colonial Advocate,* in its issue of January 28, 1828, relayed the news under the jubilant headline, "A Glorious Proof of the Effect of Petitioning".

For Mackenzie the whole affair was a splendid personal triumph; furthermore, it was a vindication of all his criticisms of the York government establishment—in his mind the very same crew that had wrecked his newspaper office. His belief that Strachan, Robinson, Macaulay, and Company stood for injustice and corruption now became almost an obsession. For Peregrine Maitland and his colonial supporters, who had played down American discontent as having been created by a factious minority that was unworthy of attention, the Randal mission was an intolerable rebuff. British instructions had been followed in making up the 1826 bill and the Colonial Office veto had made them lose face.

Back in 1826 John Strachan had suffered the uncomfortable six-week trip overseas to attend to "official business" for his Church and his friend the Lieutenant-Governor. Mackenzie, always suspicious of Strachan and his quiet behind-the-scenes way of operating, was sure something was brewing when the visit lasted for more than a year.

News of Strachan's activities was sent home to Canadian Presbyterians by their brethren in England. They were seeking verification of statistics that Strachan had presented to the Colonial Office in the form of an "Ecclesiastical Chart" showing that his Church was ministering to more people in the province than other denominations and therefore deserved preferential financial support from Britain. Presbyterians, and Methodists as well, were quick to point out that their strength had been downgraded by errors and omissions in the chart. By the time Strachan returned in the fall of 1827, everyone knew about his lobbying—Mackenzie had seen to that. And his *Colonial Advocate* accused Strachan of deliberately lying.

Strachan added fuel to the fire by announcing happily that he had obtained a charter for a Church-run university, which had always been his dream for Upper Canada. It was to be called King's College and he was to be president. In keeping with the English university tradition of Church sponsorship, the bishop and other churchmen were to be on the board. The faculty would be called upon to pledge allegiance to the Church of England, though Strachan had worked hard to have King's College open to any student in the province regardless of religious affiliation.

Instead of being universally hailed for his achievement, Strachan was denounced. The non-sectarian North American competitive society was far from willing to accept a traditional British institution, and Mackenzie vehemently opposed the university and its Church-dominated faculty in the columns of his paper. He declared that it was "one of the most obnoxious chartered institutions on earth, namely a bigoted seminary of learning." Of course he was joined by many Methodists, Presbyterians, free-thinkers, and even some Church of England adherents who doubted the validity of the Church's privileged position.

Unlike Macaulay, Strachan would not take part in a public debate, though Mackenzie tried hard enough to goad him. In the January 10, 1828 issue of the *Colonial Advocate* he printed an invented account of Strachan talking to himself.

Alas and lack a day! Why did I leave off the pious habits of my early youth to turn state physician, bank director, grand vizier, priest and politician? Why did I lose my integrity and forget the pious injunctions I received in old Aberdeen? Oh John Robinson, John Robinson, the chart lies heavy on my conscience.

Strachan ignored this—and frustrated Mackenzie, who had a compulsion to be noticed.

Egerton Ryerson joined in the attack. Almost every week throughout the summer of 1828 there appeared in the *Colonial Advocate* calmly worded public letters from Ryerson to Strachan intelligently attempting to refute every claim made by the Archdeacon of York. They were a continuation of his attack on the privileges sought by the Church of England and his one-sided debate with Strachan that he had published in 1826. Mackenzie noted in the July 22 *Advocate* that Ryerson "addresses himself to the task of detecting and exposing the fallacies and discrepancies" of Strachan's public statements. The editor said that the "tribunal of public opinion will give its fair and unbiased verdict."

Political writing and petitioning had whetted in Mackenzie an appetite for action that his newspaper alone could not satisfy. Elections were set for the summer of 1828 and Mackenzie decided to try for a seat in the Assembly. There, he reasoned, he would be able to conduct a more effective crusade for reform.

Under the present system the Legislative Council—of which John Strachan was a member—could ignore any bills passed by the Assembly. It was often justified in doing so, for the House was noted for its incompetence and qualified men were slow to offer themselves for office. Even Mackenzie was contemptuous of Assemblymen and had written that "many of these Legislators are qualified to sign their names, but as to framing and carrying through a bill on any subject what-

Egerton Ryerson

John Strachan

Robert Baldwin

John Beverley Robinson

ever, the half of them wisely never attempted such a hercu-
lean task." Any reprobate could stand for election and have a
good chance of succeeding. As there were no hard-and-fast
party lines, candidates could promise voters anything and
then, once elected, allow personal expediency to dictate their
policies in the Assembly. Mackenzie vowed in the *Advocate*
that he would be a worthy candidate: he was both independent and capable of objective criticism of all men and issues.

On December 17, 1827 he expressed his intention to run
for office in the election of the coming summer and promised
to try to maintain untarnished his principles of service to
the people of the province: "I have no end in view but the
well-being of the people at large—no ambition to serve but
that of contributing to the happiness and prosperity of our
common country." Mackenzie chose the riding of York
County, which lay north from Lot (Queen) Street and extended almost to Lake Simcoe.* It was natural that he should
turn to farmers for support. They were self-reliant and more
free of government patronage than town people and would
judge their political candidate accordingly.

Also running for election in York County were Jesse
Ketchum and James Small. And at the last moment Robert
Baldwin joined the fray. Two of the four would be declared
elected.

Forty-six-year-old Ketchum was American by birth, but by
virtue of his twenty-nine-year residence and his wealth, he
ranked as one of York's first citizens. Although uneducated,
he was a successful businessman—he had tannery establishments in both York and Buffalo—and a reform-minded acti-
vist. He was highly regarded by the lower classes of York
because of his philanthropies—he gave both time and money

* York County comprised present-day Peel, York, and Ontario Counties.

to the welfare of the community. John Carroll wrote that "it would take volumes to tell of all the poor boys and destitute families he befriended, helping them in the very best of ways by giving them employment and putting them in a way to create for themselves a home." Though Ketchum supported the Church of England, he opened his home to travelling Methodist preachers and was largely responsible for establishing the first Presbyterian church in York. Even if the haughty Sir Peregrine Maitland considered him "an illiterate man, and by no means spoken of as a British subject", the rural voters knew him as *their* man.

James Small had been one of the seconds in the Jarvis-Ridout duel; he was also one of the two men who had pleaded Mackenzie's case before the court in the press-types incident. Politically he was a moderate—he considered issues on their relative merits—but education, upbringing, and profession made lawyer Small seem to Mackenzie to be Tory. The *Advocate* of April 3 published a list of his family connections that proved conclusively to Mackenzie that this political opponent *must* be a Tory: Small's father, brother, and his wife's father and two brothers (Ridouts) were listed as employed in various government-related jobs. Mackenzie characterized Small's moderate stance as political opportunism—the Tory pretending to be a friend of the people. During the election campaign Mackenzie published rumours that Small had used his legal profession to defraud a client—a Mr Hogg who farmed north of York on Yonge Street. The resulting adverse publicity was designed to hurt Small's chances.

Twenty-four-year-old Robert Baldwin was the son of William Warren Baldwin, a prominent doctor, lawyer, and former Assemblyman. Educated by John Strachan, the young Baldwin ultimately became a renowned Reformer and a leader of the Canadian government, but to Mackenzie he was simply an establishment lawyer. "Do you know anything about young Mr Baldwin?" Francis Collins asked Mackenzie at a meeting called to choose a candidate to run against Attorney-General Robinson in the Town of York. "No," answered Mackenzie, "I know nothing about him—but I will oppose him because I do not like the family."

The race was on. Not only was Mackenzie endeavouring to defeat Small and Baldwin in York County, but, through the *Colonial Advocate,* he took it upon himself to oppose and criticize all those he considered to be the most prominent pro-government candidates in other ridings. On May 8, 1828 he gave notice that, at a cost of $200 to himself, he was printing for distribution throughout all constituencies a pamphlet entitled "The Legislative Black List of Upper Canada; or Official Corruption and Hypocrisy Unmasked". He described the publication as his gift "to the Free and Independent Electors of Upper Canada on the second Anniversary of the destruction of his Newspaper Office", thereby giving notice that he was taking special aim at the York ruling clique.

From May 29 to July 10 excerpts from the pamphlet appeared in the *Advocate.* Mackenzie listed and discussed the voting patterns of selected Assemblymen on bills—dating as far back as 1810—that he considered to have been most important to the colony. The bills were numbered 1 to 105 and given labels (79—the Alien Bill; 81—$200,000 loan to the Welland Canal; 91—"The Humbug University, or Strachan As He Is"). Mackenzie's blacklist was designed to show that elected legislators could not be trusted to vote as their constituents might expect. In other words, the members of the present Assembly had not been representing the people;

THE LEGISLATIVE
Black List,
OF
UPPER CANADA;
OR OFFICIAL CORRUPTION AND HYPOCRISY UNMASKED.

By W. L. MACKENZIE, Editor of the Advocate.

MOTTO.

The British Government wanted to tax the Americans, without letting them send Members to Parliament. The people of America resisted ; and in the House of Lords, *Lord Chatham*, the father of Pitt, said, that they had "a right to resist," and that *he* "rejoiced that they had resisted."

"He who is taxed without his consent is a slave. He may call himself what he will ; but, if he has no voice in the making of the laws, by which he is liable to be punished, and by which his property is taken away and applied to the use of others, he is, to all intents and purposes, a slave."

In Upper Canada, not one fifth part of the actual revenue raised by taxes, upon the people, is at the disposal of their representatives. They are taxed without their consent, and these taxes are appropriated, by the King's representative, without their authority.

Mr. Huskisson's conduct, as colonial minister, promises well. But it will be time enough to give the British government credit for constitutional conduct towards Upper Canada, when the system is changed. Another revolution in America may be prevented by a due observance of the signs of the times ; but if it break out, perhaps the fleets and armies of England, with all the Brunswickers, Hessians, and other German mercenaries, which her gold could hire, would not quell it. A conflagration may be prevented at commencement, by the prudence of one person ; but when it has spread itself and gathered strength, who shall set bounds to its fury?

"*Nunc aut Nunquam.*" (*Now or never!*)—KILMORTY.

THE LIBEL.
VALUABLE REPORT ON THE CONDUCT OF THE CROWN LAWYERS.

Always anxious to inform our readers of the most important proceedings of the Colonial Legislature, we hasten to direct their attention to the report of a select committee of the House of Assembly on the petition of Mr. Forsyth, of Niagara Falls, loudly complaining of the conduct of the crown officers, and of a defective and partial administration of justice. The report speaks a language not to be misunderstood, and we trust that a perusal of it will serve to stir up the dormant energies of the wholesome part of the population, and induce them to exert themselves manfully to 'clear the House of Assembly next election, of the Attorney General, Speaker Willson, Jonas, David, and Charles Jones, Messrs. Burnham, Coleman, Scollick, Gordon, McDonell, Beasley, Clark, McLean, Vankoughnett, and the whole of that ominous nest of Unclean birds which have so long lain close under the wings of a spendthrift executive, and (politically to speak) actually preyed upon the very vitals of the country they ought to have loved cherished and protected. No wonder it is that parliament should find its energies all but paralyzed, when such an accumulation of corrupt materials is left UNSWEPT WITH THE BESOM OF THE PEOPLE'S WRATH from out of these halls they have so long and so shamefully "degled with their abominations."—[From the Colonial Advocate, of April 3rd.)

"MAHLON BURWELL said, *he cared not for the people's opinions*. As a proof "of Mr. Gourlay's evil intentions he instanced the expression in one of his addresses, "'*surely when the blood of Britons has ebbed to the lowest mark, it will learn to flow* "*again*,' which he undoubtedly took to mean, that it should flow in the field ; and "that it was an excitement to rebellion."

No. 6. *Places of Profit, Honour, and Emolument held by some of the members of the present or last House of Assembly, or by candidates for the legislature.*

John B. Robinson,—Attorney General ; Colonel of Militia ; King's College Counsellor ; Welland Canal Director ; Hospital Trustee ; Allegiance Commissioner ; School Trustee ;

Z. Burnham,—J. P. ; District Treasurer ; Allegiance Commissioner ; School Trustee ; Lieutenant Colonel of Militia ;

John Clark,—J. P. ; Major of Militia ; Ex. Canal Commissioner ; Assistant to Adjutant General ;

This excerpt from Mackenzie's "Black List of Upper Canada" appeared in the Colonial Advocate on May 29, 1828.

most of their votes reflected the wishes of the governing clique.

First publication of the blacklist virtually coincided with the publication of an article entitled "Valuable Report on the Conduct of Crown Lawyers" that called upon people to cast out of the Assembly

the whole of the ominous nest of unclean birds which have so long lain close under the wings of a spendthrift executive, and (politically to speak) actually preyed upon the very vitals of the country they ought to have loved and cherished and protected.

This passage was considered libellous and a suit was brought against Mackenzie. Early in May 1828 he was called to court to answer a libel charge but the case was postponed and Mackenzie was released on $800 bail.* Mackenzie vowed to publish the offensive passage in every issue of the *Advocate* and give the electorate a chance to decide, in the light of the blacklist, whether the accusations against the Assemblymen were true or false.

The election, held in mid-July, produced a devastating reaction against many members of the previous Assembly. With the controversies over the Alien Bill, Strachan's "Ecclesiastical Chart" and university, and the blacklist's revelations, there were enough solid issues to make any voter wary of the power of the existing government. Robinson was re-elected by his town constituents, but only two others who had supported the Alien Bill were returned to office. Not only were all reform Assemblymen re-elected, but they were reinforced by like-minded additions, including Jesse Ketchum and William Lyon Mackenzie. The character of the new Assembly was distinctly reformist.

* On April 2, 1829 the Lieutenant-Governor ordered the charge dropped.

Until the summer of 1828 elections to the Assembly had been based on personal popularity, or on the extent to which a candidate was favoured and supported by government officials; within the Assembly votes were cast on the basis of individual conscience. But now party lines began to develop in a province that previously had not known them. As a result of the election issues some men began to identify themselves as "Reformers", in official opposition to the government. John Rolph, Marshall Spring Bidwell, and Dr William Warren Baldwin began to consult each other on goals and the strategy necessary to achieve them. Mackenzie was not part of this group, however; he was a political independent and preferred to act on his own.

Like the Tories, Mackenzie was a firm believer in the British monarchy; but he also believed passionately in change, while they did not. Because he had come to Upper Canada many years after the War of 1812, he did not experience the fervent British nationalism or the hostility to Americans that coloured the thinking of Tories as a result of that conflict.

About all that Mackenzie had in common with Baldwin, Bidwell, and Rolph was his desire for change and his lack of anti-Americanism. These Reformers were well-established professional men. They could meet the Tories, socially and in political debate, on the same footing; Mackenzie could not. Furthermore, unlike Dr Baldwin, he was not a political theorist; he had no plan. His approach was instinctive and direct. His first concern was people and he desired, as he often said, only the immediate welfare of his constituents. He believed that the justice of his cause and the persuasiveness of his arguments, combined with his dedication and hard work, would enable him to bring this about on his own.

Mackenzie was becoming aware of his political potential. As an Assemblyman he was no longer merely a journalistic name-caller and muckraker but was now in a position to have his political and economic ideas listened to and taken seriously. He was not popular, however, nor was he even appreciated. In the election of 1828 his margin of victory over James Small was narrow and he was well behind Jesse Ketchum. Yet his technique of visiting the people in small towns and isolated settlements, of recording his findings and publicizing them through the *Colonial Advocate,* and of encouraging petitions and united action, created a strong impression. His attempts to instil some participatory democracy into the backward province could augur well for his constituents—and for all the people of Upper Canada.

3

Appeals to the People

The *Colonial Advocate*, now published with the help of apprentices, was still very much Mackenzie's voice. It rolled off the press week by week every Thursday: challenging, irritating, and occasionally amusing, though now lacking its pre-election viciousness. Mackenzie continued to goad the government establishment. Reflecting upon persistent rumours in the summer of 1828 that Maitland would soon be leaving, Mackenzie wrote:

We consider Sir P. Maitland a weak and feeble minded man, and although we would greatly rejoice to see him removed out of this country to Jamaica or some other West India plantation, yet would we pity the people whose fate it might be to endure so heavy a burden upon the energies of their country.

Indeed, Maitland did leave (he was promoted to Governor of Nova Scotia) and was replaced by Sir John Colborne.

The Reformers optimistically hoped that the new Lieutenant-Governor would be open-minded and fair, but Mackenzie was skeptical. Colborne "is an entire stranger among us", he wrote in the *Colonial Advocate*, "and with Doctor Strachan and his scholars for counsellors, it would surely be marvellous if he went a step right." Colborne and his wife—with a household consisting of four daughters, four sons, and eight servants—arrived in York in October.

Meanwhile other changes in the colony's governmental hierarchy were in the offing and John Beverley Robinson—now a fellow Assemblyman with Mackenzie, much to the latter's distaste—became the subject of the next rumour. In November Mackenzie heard that Robinson was likely to be appointed Chief Justice. His contempt knew no bounds: "[Robinson] is deservedly the most unpopular man in the colony, next to Boulton and Archdeacon Strachan." The *Colonial Advocate* spitefully listed all those who had voted for Robinson in the last York town election, in categories chosen to illustrate why. In the first class there were 38 who Mackenzie claimed were dependent on the government for "their daily bread". There were 18 office-holders in the second class, and in the last group were 53 masons, tavern-keepers, and tradesmen etc. who more or less relied on the bank and the government to support their businesses. When Robinson received the appointment, Mackenzie wrote: "It is very evident that the British government, either from ignorance or design, treat the people here as *something below* the rank of freemen."

The Assembly opened in January 1829. The reform-minded members who had been elected the previous summer lacked leadership and party discipline. Instead of organizing themselves to tackle any one problem, they presented the Legislative Council and the new Lieutenant-Governor with a continual stream of accusations and demands. Marshall Spring Bidwell, an educated and moderate man, was not able to instil a spirit of unity and steadfastness of purpose in the Assemblymen because he was the Speaker and officially neutral. The competent but unassertive Robert Baldwin, who won Robinson's town seat in a by-election in 1830, was a dedicated Reformer but unwilling to take any initiative. John Rolph (who was now a practising doctor) was a gifted speaker but he was indecisive. There were no other potential leaders.

There was no Tory party either—just a small group of men in the Assembly bound together by family background, education, or business interests who knew how to co-operate to achieve mutual goals or to thwart opposition. After the War of 1812 their influence was paramount in promoting the Alien Act and restrictions on Americans. They had united in 1819 to force the expulsion of Robert Gourlay, a Scottish land developer who had stirred up discontent in the province against the government. And they shared a dislike of the non-Tory members of the Assembly, most of whom seemed to them to be an incoherent rabble, uneducated and uncouth.

The Reform Assembly of 1829 made an auspicious start. By a vote of 37 to 1 they carried the address opposing the Speech from the Throne and showed that at least they were united in their distaste for the office of the Lieutenant-Governor. However, the forty-eight Assemblymen from around the province soon settled in to enjoy town life for three months; most of the debating and committee work was left to the few eager and capable members. "During the whole of five or six speeches", commented John Langton, "not a single member appeared to think of anything but his own business; and when one speaker sat down and another arose, very few even condescended to look up from their papers to see who it might be."

Mackenzie was an energetic, tireless worker. In the first two weeks of the session he was in the forefront as a mover of resolutions and an originator of committees. A resolution on the first day of business, January 9, "that the president and cashier of the Bank of Upper Canada be required to make a return to this House of the funds and property of the Bank", indicated his belief that the Assembly should know all the facts about the bank—now withheld—since the government owned one quarter of its shares. His motions for the establishment of two standing committees on agriculture and commerce were adopted, as well as his demands for select committees on the Post Office and on privilege. Mackenzie became the chairman of the latter two and his reports were ready within two months.

In the interval he brought forward private petitions to deal with stray cattle, improve the poor conditions of roads and bridges, and provide British periodicals for the parliamentary library. It was as if he felt that by hard work he could singlehandedly change the abuses and inefficiency he so passionately hated.

The Post Office committee asked for "a domestic establishment under the direction of an officer accountable to the Legislature of this Province for his every act". In the light of Mackenzie's past faith in Britain, this was a radical request, a complete departure from his earlier recommendation to lower postage rates by the establishment of a common legislature for all the British colonies that "could pass laws binding on the whole in ... cases such as the Post Office". But Mackenzie now thought that if reforms could not be made in the British system, then the people of Upper Canada should take matters into their own hands. Though a Post Office under Canadian control would not show a profit—as it now did for Britain—it would provide better service.

The Privilege committee was investigating patronage and suspected conflicts of interest in local government. How and why were government officials appointed, especially at election time? The committee claimed that "limits were put on political freedom" because of the fees charged by the returning officer. The specific target of the committee was Sheriff Jarvis, who had been the returning officer for the town and county of York in the recent election.

Elections were held over a period of four to six days, with the voters coming long distances to a central or convenient place in the riding (usually a tavern) to declare their choice publicly. Candidates provided liquor—unofficially, of course —and were always on hand to electioneer and harangue the doubtful. Expenses for printing, stationery, and fees for the poll clerk, returning officer, and police constable (elections were heated and sometimes violent) were charged by the returning officer to the candidates. The committee reported that £21 was demanded of each candidate after the last York County election, and complained that only the wealthy could afford to run for office. Jarvis, pleading on his own behalf, told the privilege committee that his personal fee as returning officer of a guinea a day per candidate was small compensation for the "anxiety, care, diligence, and study necessarily attendant upon the execution of so arduous a duty".

As Tory Jarvis was the sheriff, critical committee members felt that he was a threat to candidates not liked by the government. His very presence could intimidate voters and "encourage" them to vote for those favoured by the existing government establishment. The committee set down the facts as they saw them but offered no solutions. They could only report that they trusted "the wisdom of the Legislature . . . [to] provide a remedy for any abuses that may be found to exist".

This happened often, for there were many grievances and few solutions. To the frustration of the Assembly, when it did pass bills an unsympathetic Legislative Council usually (though not always) rejected them: fifty-three were defeated in 1829-30 alone. One bill that was turned down requested that clergymen of denominations other than the Church of England share and be paid for chaplain duties to the Assembly. Mackenzie claimed that the impervious Legislative Council was "the most wearisome piece of lumber ever invented to clog the wheels of a youthful state". He in turn was referred to by council members as "the little manikin from York".

The more committees Mackenzie initiated and worked for, the more discouraged he became. "The present system is too corrupt to last long," he prophesied; "its rottenness will in the end cause it to fall to pieces." He complained in the Assembly, at meetings, and in his paper. "The people have no check upon the public expenditures—no remedy for abuses, but to bear them. England . . . means us well—but she is not at our door, and justice even in England is a costly commodity." For the high-strung Mackenzie peace and tranquillity were not possible even at night. "I can truly say that I have come from the House night after night, at 8 or 10 or 12 p.m. after a twelve hours' attendance, so tired and worn out that when I went to bed I could not sleep for perfect fatigue."

In the late spring and early summer of 1829 Mackenzie visited New York, Washington, Philadelphia, and other American cities to buy books. While in the United States he thought he discovered why the authorities in York feared the naturalization of Americans. It was because "they have such a good system of government that they would never want to give it up for the antiquated British monarchical system." He hit upon a solution to his frustrations as an Assemblyman: do away with dependence upon Great Britain; draw up a written constitution to which the legislature would have to conform and against which no council would dare act.

Without waiting to return home, he published letters in the *National Gazette* of Philadelphia (which were soon copied in the *Advocate*). One of them stated that the people of Upper Canada were

denied the blessings of representative government, denied equal justice, denied the management of internal affairs, cursed with three church establishments, while education languishes, and the country is daily more and more impoverished by rapacious office-holders. They hold what little freedom they possess merely on sufferance.

He went on to give an idealized picture of American society, which to him appeared to lack social classes. "The only aristocracy to be found here is the nobility of talent, character, or wealth," Mackenzie rhapsodized. "Here you may propose absolute monarchy or set forth the advantage of extreme democracy, advocate and lecture all who will hear you in favour of atheism, infidelity or deism or against them . . . *no one will disturb you."*

Such views were highly unacceptable to the many Britons who had emigrated to Canada with the intention of remaining in a British system of government and society; they were not prepared to accept Mackenzie's exaggerated claims for the United States made on the basis of one short visit. Colborne and many other prominent government figures, firmly anti-American, were even more incensed by Mackenzie's next utterance—another letter in the Philadelphia newspaper, this time comparing governors.

John Andrew Shulze is proud of the honour of governing a million and upwards of his countrymen of Pennsylvania, with a salary of $4,000 a year. John Colborne, for military service done to the aristocracy of England, has consigned to him the *people and government of Upper Canada for seven years more or less, at per invoice $20,000 per annum[!]. Shulze was born in Pennsylvania and means to leave his bones there. Colborne, and the half-pay officers about him, must at a month's warning sell out and depart with their winnings to old England and be seen no more after eating us up, bones and all.*

Mackenzie was dubbed "our Yankee minister".

During the fall of 1829 and the first half of 1830 Mackenzie was busy making inquiries and reporting on his committee work. These were quiet months for the *Colonial Advocate*. It was mainly devoted to articles culled from other papers and journals. Spread out over several issues were such fillers as "A Catechism of Education"—a rather pretentious question-and-answer discussion of the learning experience—and a complete treatise on horses. Sam Patch, a wandering stunt man, made spectacular news by executing a daring and successful leap over Niagara Falls, which was duly described. Several issues later an obituary reported that he died while drunkenly attempting a repeat performance. Occasionally Mackenzie squeezed in some conundrums, which illustrate his sense of humour (or rather lack of one):

Question: If a woman were to change her sex, of what religion would she be?
Answer: He-then.
Question: What makes all women alike?
Answer: The dark.
Question: Where did Noah strike the first nail in the ark?
Answer: On the head.

In the summer of 1830 an annual grant of £100 from the government made it possible for some prominent Tories to organize an agricultural society. The general public was invited to join by paying a subscription fee and a meeting was held to draw up the rules of the association. Mary O'Brien, whose husband Edward was a founding member, wrote in a letter home to England that the farmers "came forward in tolerable numbers with their Mackenzie". Jarvis, the treasurer, asked Mackenzie to subscribe. Only those who had paid were allowed to speak "or have anything to say in forming the by-laws or framing the constitution", but this rule did not prevent Mackenzie from standing up and haranguing the gathering. He was asked politely to sit down and be quiet but he ignored the request and went on speaking. Many were annoyed and shouted "Turn him out!" Mackenzie went on, oblivious to the consternation of the Tories. John Elmsley and others then "laid hold of him and . . . shoved him to the door and out of it, fastening [it] on the inside. . . . The little blackguard then, like a spoilt and ill-behaved baby, kept thumping at the door."

On August 12, 1830, news of the death of George IV was published in the *Advocate*. William IV was proclaimed the new king, and in accordance with British tradition the legislature was dissolved. New elections were to be held in the early fall.

Mackenzie, as usual, threw all his energies into the campaign. His official advertisement stated his platform; there were no fancy promises. "Of my conduct in the Legislature you have been witnesses—be now also its judges."

In the preceding year and a half there had been no scandals or political issues with which to discredit the government, as there had been in 1828. The king was represented by a capable man, in the person of John Colborne, who was genuinely trying to understand and serve the province. Although opposed to democracy and strongly in favour of monarchical and upper-class government, Lieutenant-Governor Colborne was much more tactful and aware of the importance of public opinion than his predecessor. He shelved the unpopular plans for Strachan's King's College* and established a grammar school—later known as Upper Canada College—to improve the quality of secondary-school education in the province. Colborne also suggested to the Colonial Office that the Legislative Council should be open to a wider membership to de-emphasize the York clique. He told the Colonial Office that the Church would be strengthened if the Reverend John Strachan could be persuaded to step down from either of the appointed councils. Moreover he saw that the Methodists' "saddlebag" type of ministry was very effective in reaching pioneer communities and recommended that the Church of England also appoint travelling ministers.

The Reformers in the Assembly had been unable to focus the attention of the population on the few economic or political problems that could be solved; aside from a multitudinous list of grievances they could produce nothing better than noisy talk. The veto power of the Legislative Council made a Tory Assembly a necessity if any economic progress was to take place, and since the Tories were mostly businessmen and people of independent means, it seemed as though they were best able to carry out beneficial planning for the province's future. By the time of the election of 1830 most of the electorate were ready to forget about democratic reforms for a while and instead try to raise the standard of living. Out of a total of fifty-four members only about seventeen Reformers were elected. Jesse Ketchum and Mac-

---

* King's College was eventually built in 1842-3, on a site chosen by Strachan (that of the present Legislative Building in Queen's Park). It became the University of Toronto in 1854.

kenzie were re-elected for York County, but Robert Baldwin was defeated in the York town riding—by Sheriff Jarvis.

The defeat of so many reform-minded men had much less significance for Mackenzie than the fact that he himself had been successful, and with an increased majority. His post-mortem on the election expressed his dissatisfaction with under-representation in his riding. Statistics showed the population of York County, at 23,388, to be nine times that of York town, and yet it had only twice the number of members (i.e. two). Mackenzie suggested in the *Advocate* that from six to eight was more realistic. He also thought that the whole election process could be conducted with less trouble and expense, and might even encourage independence of voting, if votes were cast by ballot at centres in every township.

At the time of the opening of the new Assembly early in January the *Advocate* was full of "GLORIOUS NEWS". The British Tory party had been forced to resign and a reforming Whig ministry had taken over parliament. "The people will have their own day," rejoiced the exuberant Mackenzie, who expected that the Whigs would gladly support reform in Upper Canada.

In the first few months of 1831 progressive changes were made in the government of Upper Canada on the initiative of the Colonial Office. The Legislative Council was enlarged to include men—most of them Tories—from Prescott, Cobourg, Grimsby, Fort Erie, Kingston, and Ottawa, as well as several from York. To give the colony more independence, Britain put in the hands of the Assembly control of Upper Canada's share of the revenue raised from customs duties collected at Quebec. In return it had to grant the Lieutenant-Governor a permanent civil list, which guaranteed certain government officials* their salaries without Assembly interference.**

On the very first day of the session Mackenzie moved two resolutions and gave notice of seven more; and the predominantly Tory Assembly appeared willing to appease him. A week later—over the objections of Attorney-General Henry Boulton and other extreme Tories—he asked for and received approval to set up a select committee on the State of Representation of the people in the Assembly. During the winter session and an unusual second session in the fall the Assembly kept Mackenzie busy—and, it hoped, out of the way—on committees investigating currency, prisons, roads and bridges, the Bank of Upper Canada, justice, and the Welland Canal. Many of these committees he himself had proposed.

Throughout 1831 Mackenzie remained totally wrapped up in politics. His *Colonial Advocate* was mostly an echo of the Assembly's official *Journal of Proceedings*. It kept pioneer readers informed of all committee reports and gave a picture of Assembly deliberations—coloured by Mackenzie's editorializing—that was not found in most other colonial newspapers, many of which were nothing but gossip sheets. Hardworking settlers could read that the Welland Canal was a monument to "ignorance, folly, cupidity, united with avarice"; that the Bank of Upper Canada was "a monopoly" and "very dangerous to civil liberty—always siding with the few against the many"; and that roads and bridges throughout the province were "in a wretched shape". Some subscribers might

---

* The Lieutenant-Governor, judges of King's Bench, the Attorney- and Solicitor-General, five Executive Councillors, and the clerk of the Executive Council.

** Mackenzie claimed that government men were already too independent of public opinion and dubbed this the "Everlasting Salary Bill".

hesitate to accept the first two judgements at face value, but the "roads" were notorious and Mackenzie clearly knew what he was talking about when he discussed that subject. There were too few roads to begin with, and in fact none at all where surveyed rights of way bypassed unsold or reserved land.

Mackenzie's State of Representation committee, influenced by the Whig reform of election practices in England, showed that constituencies in the province were not justly represented according to population and that a redistribution of seats was necessary. The report included, in an appendix, a list of Assemblymen who also held public office—as sheriffs, judges, postmasters etc.—and their salaries. This made Attorney-General (and also Judge) Henry Boulton very angry. Opposed to the committee at the outset, he now looked for a way to retaliate.

Boulton got his chance when Mackenzie paid out of his own pocket for a privately printed *Journal* intended for his own personal distribution. This had been done by others in the past, but Mackenzie neglected to print the appendixes —containing committee reports, correspondence, and occasional directives from the Lieutenant-Governor relating to bills—that in many cases would have modified the conclusions a reader might come to regarding legislation. Henry Boulton and Christopher Hagerman introduced a breach-of-privilege motion against Mackenzie, but it was defeated 24 to 11 by a Tory Assembly that was moderate enough to avoid making an issue of his misdemeanour. Extreme Tories were forced to bide their time over a summer recess.

Throughout 1830 and 1831 Sir John Colborne had been busy promoting emigration from Britain with the result that the population of York rose from 2,860 in 1830 to 3,969 in

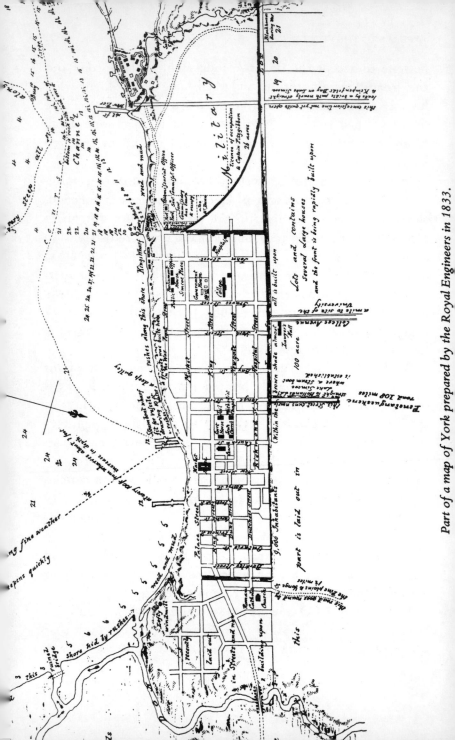

Part of a map of York prepared by the Royal Engineers in 1833.

1831, to 5,505 in 1832. Vast numbers of people thronged off the decks of the four lake steamers, and with them came new styles of life that brought marked changes to York. Any American atmosphere that had existed in York was now overshadowed by the presence of predominantly British immigrants. Of these the Irish were the most prominent and they kept the town lively. When they weren't feuding with others, they fought among themselves.

Although York was still primarily a government town, its importance as a commercial centre for the rapidly developing hinterland was increasing. Retail and growing wholesale trade drew buyers from miles around. The public marketplace, soon to be remodelled, was always full of produce: beef at three pence a pound, mutton at four pence, butter at eight pence, cheese at five; and a fat goose could be bought for two shillings. Visiting settlers, in town to trade their goods, were amazed at the seeming opulence. On Front Street, in the "new town", handsome legislative buildings were under construction (at a cost of over £10,000). Just to the north at King and Simcoe Streets, occupying four acres of landscaped property, stood Government House, the large residence of Sir John Colborne. Facing this edifice, on the north side of King Street, was Upper Canada College, built by Colborne in 1829. Even more impressive was the large Bank of Upper Canada, with its stone steps and mahogany fittings. The little Baptist chapel on Lombard Street and St Andrew's Presbyterian Church, at Church Street and Adelaide, were among the many brick buildings. The money, power, and status that were evident in York made the less fortunate and struggling farmers wonder about their place in society and whether the affluence of York was acquired at their expense.

Mackenzie—always sensitive to the plight and exasperation

The Parliament Buildings on Front Street, Toronto, 1834. Watercolour by John G. Howard.

of his farmer friends and frustrated by his lack of progress through committee work in the Assembly—decided that it was once again time to bypass the local government and appeal directly to the Colonial Office (and to the British parliament if they would listen). He called upon all settlers throughout the province to arrange local meetings and set down on paper their complaints and recommendations for improvements. Mackenzie organized the first meeting in York, and he and his supporters drew up and published a petition criticizing the upper echelon of local government. The system of appointed councils and elected Assembly, he claimed, gave a false appearance of democracy because government functioned without reference to the people's wishes —and the people were not aware of this.

A list of demands that, if met, would remedy the situation —or so Mackenzie believed—was drawn up for the king's perusal. Most were so general that they were useless. For instance Mackenzie stated that members of the Executive Council should possess the confidence of the people, by which he might have meant that they should be elected or at least represent the party that held the majority in the Assembly. He also said that the Assembly should control all revenue raised in the province, which under colonial government was not possible until a plan could be devised whereby Britain would give over all internal matters to local people while retaining control of external relations of the colony.

Throughout the late summer and early fall of 1831 Mackenzie travelled as much as possible, encouraging, supporting, and rallying the populace to press for dramatic changes in government and assuring them that these could be brought about with the help of the benevolent king. Petitions—much the same as Mackenzie's published criticism of the system of colonial government—flowed in from around the province, especially from many former Americans who had settled in Upper Canada.

When the second session of the 1831 Assembly began on November 17, Mackenzie was in high spirits. He was worked up over his travels and public meetings, over his petitions and their thousands of signatures. His enthusiasm for his cause and his hatred for the government brought about a faux pas in the December 1 *Colonial Advocate*. As he had done in the *National Gazette* of Philadelphia two years previously, he downgraded the Upper Canadian government in a superficial comparison with another—this time the government of Lower Canada.

The contrast between their executive and ours, between the material of our assembly and theirs, and between the use they make of an invaluable constitution and our abuse of it, is anything but satisfactory to the friends of freedom and social order in Upper Canada. Our representative body has degenerated into a sycophantic office for registering the decrees of as mean and mercenary an executive as was ever given as a punishment for the sins of any part of North America in the nineteenth century.

In the previous session of the Assembly many moderate Tories had tried to ignore Mackenzie whenever possible, or keep him busy on committee work; they had resisted the efforts of Boulton and Hagerman to persecute him. Their reward was a summer of public meetings in which he mocked and condemned them and their Assembly. The latest publication was an outrage—too much for the already hostile Assemblymen to bear. Mackenzie was promptly presented with a charge of libel—not to be brought before the law courts, but to be judged by the Assembly itself.

When Mackenzie was given a chance to defend himself, he stubbornly refused to back down. "Not one word do I retract!" he shouted. "I offer no apology. For what you call libel I believe to be the solemn truth, fit to be published from one end of the province to the other." On December 12, 1831, a motion for Mackenzie's expulsion was carried in the Assembly by a vote of 24 to 15. Reformers such as Bidwell gave him their support claiming that the freedom of the press was at stake, but their protests were not very convincing.

Within three weeks a by-election was held in York County to fill the vacancy created by the expulsion. The Tories put up a token resistance to Mackenzie but there was no prominent candidate willing to stand against him on such short notice. On election day, January 2, forty sleighs accompanied Mackenzie to the polls at the Red Lion Inn on Yonge Street, northeast of the toll-gate (at present-day Bloor Street). The chill of the early January frost did not keep away 119 of his electorate, and there was only one opposing vote. Sheriff Jarvis (back at his old job as returning officer), who had carefully scrutinized each voter, had to proclaim Mackenzie elected. A fervent mob escorted him in triumph to the ballroom of the Red Lion Inn and presented him with a $250 gold medal on which was inscribed "Presented to Wm. Lyon Mackenzie, Esq., by his contituents of the County of York, U.C., as a token of their approbation of his political career." On the front of the medal, encircling an emblematic thistle, rose, and shamrock, were the words, "His Majesty King William IV the People's Friend".

Mackenzie was driven back to York in a double-decker sleigh pulled by four teams of horses. One hundred and thirty-four sleighs progressed down Yonge Street—over ninety more than had accompanied Mackenzie up the same

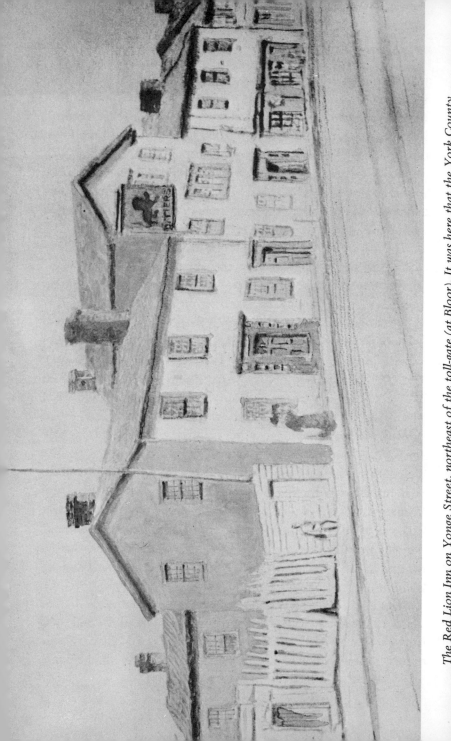

The Red Lion Inn on Yonge Street, northeast of the toll-gate (at Bloor). It was here that the York County

route earlier on the way to the polls—and one proudly bore a crimson flag proclaiming the motto "Freedom of the Press". Bagpipe music and whoops of joy filled the crisp air. That day was one of the happiest in Mackenzie's life—a thrilling high point in his career and fortunes. He was sure of himself and basked in public acclaim for deeds despised by the ruling class. At home that evening the hero of the boisterous York constituency was in high spirits over his impressive victory. Mackenzie threw his medal in the air and his wig on the floor; then, turning, he flung his arms round his mother's neck and kissed her.

Several days after his election victory the unrepentant Mackenzie published a violent attack on Sir John Colborne—a partial reiteration of his January 2 election speech. Again he was charged with libel* and the Assembly prepared to oust him once more. Prominent Reformers in the House were less sympathetic this time. Peter Perry, the outstanding economic mind of the Reformers, attempted to head off the expulsion with a compromise motion that would have rebuked Mackenzie but not made a martyr of him. This sensible idea was lost, however, in the face of the headstrong hatred of the Tories for William Lyon Mackenzie. They declared that he could not sit in the present session and expelled him a second time on January 7, 1832 for

gross, scandalous, and malicious libels . . . endeavouring . . . to cause His Majesty's subjects of this Province to believe that the majority of their representatives should be held in execration and abhorrence by posterity, as enemies to the liberties of the people they represent.

The Assembly's action merely increased Mackenzie's popularity with the people.

* His election speech of January 2 was cited as one piece of evidence.

From January 30 to February 4 in York County farmers, tradesmen, and mechanics came out for the second time in a month—some walking a round trip of 100 miles—to re-elect their man, who they thought had been unjustly convicted for proclaiming their rights. Mackenzie received 628 votes, 532 more than his nearest rival. (This time competition had come forward in the person of Tory Sam Washburn and moderate James Small.* Washburn bitterly withdrew early in the voting because of lack of support.) Mackenzie was completely carried away by his success and the emotion of his followers. His victory speech was 9,000 words long. In it he spitefully condemned Colborne (even though the Lieutenant-Governor had been against his expulsion and had tried to counsel the Tories to temper their reaction to Mackenzie). He "wishes to keep you ignorant in order that you may be enslaved," Mackenzie warned.

The Assembly would not accept Mackenzie's re-election and another motion for his expulsion was brought forward on the grounds that he was ineligible to sit in the present session. Attorney-General Boulton agreed with Perry that this was nonsense. Nonetheless the expulsion was carried out.

In the past the Reformers might have moderated Mackenzie, but this series of harsh actions against him had brought him sufficient support throughout the province that he could now act confidently and successfully without Perry and Ketchum. York County belonged to "Little Mac".

In the winter of 1832 Mackenzie stirred up interest and backing for a projected trip to England, during which he intended to present the previous summer's petitions to the

---

* Small publicized the fact that he was not really opposed to Mackenzie but had offered his services in order that the riding might be represented by a Reformer. He assumed that the Assembly was not going to allow Mackenzie back in.

British government. He took his ideas and beliefs to the market square, where he spoke to farmers from the surrounding countryside on the subject of their rights and the need for determined action against the machinations of the Tories. A witness to these gatherings, as reported by Kathleen and Robina Lizars in their *Humours of '37*, testified to his impact.

Every market day, when business was all done before the farmers went home, there would be a crowd around him as he talked from the top of a wagon. He made great speeches, I can tell you. I happened to be there once through a person who was staying in his house. We turned down by the church and waited at the market below King Street where he was standing in a wagon talking and you should have seen how the people listened.

By March 1832 York was in an uproar. As if his attacks on the government establishment were not enough, Mackenzie was now proposing to visit England with petitions bearing thousands of signatures of disgruntled settlers. Rival Tory groups held meetings, in town and throughout the province, to proclaim their loyalty and satisfaction with the status quo. On March 12 Bishop Alexander Macdonell headed a meeting of town Roman Catholics to gather petitions opposing Mackenzie's. The editor and his supporters occupied the meeting room in the Union Hotel before the Roman Catholics could assemble and refused to leave. (An Upper Canadian sit-in!)

No doubt with some exaggeration, the *Canadian Freeman* —whose Roman Catholic editor, Francis Collins, reported the affair—gave this account of Mackenzie's fate:

Two manly Irishmen remained in the room and little Mackenzie rose up on a bench to address his mob—when one of the Irishmen put his finger to the butt of Mackenzie's wig

*and pitched him, as a boy would a shuttlecock, from one end
of the room to the other! Little Mac fell, we hear, like a
cat—all fours, and the wig went under a bench. . . . The little
man gathered himself up, picked up his wig, and ran for his
life. As he arrived at the head of the stairs, the second boy
met him and gave him, we hear, a kick which landed him at
the hall door, thus saving him the trouble of walking downstairs. Although about fifty of his mob were present, not one
of them durst lift a hand.*

When the Mackenzie supporters refused to vacate the
premises, the denominational meeting moved to Macdonell's
room in the hotel. There a series of resolutions was passed,
"approving the upright conduct and liberal views of Sir John
Colborne, and disapproving of the misrepresentations of Mackenzie's faction".

Shortly after the Union Hotel incident Mackenzie was
present at a public meeting in the Tory community of Hamilton. It degenerated into a stormy debate on procedure. The
next day rumours were heard of a plot to take his life, or at
least to maim him. The brash editor and people's politician
declined protection and advice to leave town early and declared his intention of departing by the 11 p.m. stage.

That evening, as he sat upstairs in a friend's house writing,
two men came into the room. One of them, William Kerr,
was justice of the peace, a member of the Assembly, and a
government canal manager. He appeared friendly enough and
made a half-joking comment about the papers Mackenzie was
working on. "Well, have you got all your grievances redressed
at last?" he asked. Kerr suggested that they go downstairs, as
he wanted to say something personal to Mackenzie. Down
they went, Mackenzie holding a candle to light the way.

When they reached the ground floor Kerr opened the front

door. Pointing to Mackenzie, he called out: "This is your man!" Immediately Mackenzie was seized by his coat collar and grabbed from the other side by Kerr. His candle was dashed to the ground and several assailants struggled to pull him towards the greater darkness of the street. Mackenzie shrieked "Murder!" He was struck a blow with a cudgel, kicked, and dragged off into the night. Only the timely appearance of friends saved him from further harm. They chased everyone away except Kerr, who stayed under the pretense of helping Mackenzie. The victim bled profusely from a cut in the face and a bang on the head, and his chest hurt. "I was very unwell all next day, but able to sit up. I was a ghastly spectacle to look upon; and for months after I felt the effects of the blows and bruises."

Mackenzie's frequent charges about the corruption of the judiciary were borne out when Kerr was brought to trial, for he escaped with only a small fine and a reprimand. Tory and anti-Mackenzie sympathies were quite evident in the decision of the government-appointed judge; an extreme Reformer who had committed such an atrocity probably would have been jailed.

After Macdonell's meeting of March 12 the Protestants and Roman Catholics of York decided to show their combined support of the government. An invitation was extended to every male inhabitant of the town to come to a "Great Meeting" that Mackenzie was organizing. They would demonstrate to the world, once and for all, the relative power of Tories and Reformers. At noon on March 23, four days after the Hamilton incident, Mackenzie was back in York ready to face the meeting, which was to be held in front of the Court House. Both Tories and Reformers had come out in force and were well prepared for action. Mackenzie's side claimed later

NEWMARKET MAIL STAGE.

WILLIAM GARBUTT, having taken the contract for carrying His Majesty's Mails between York and Newmarket, for the next four years, respectfully informs the public that THE MAIL STAGE will start from Joseph Bloor's Hotel, York, on Mondays and Thursdays, at 12 o'clock, noon, and arrive at nine o'clock, the same evening in Newmarket;—and will leave Mr. Barber's Tavern, Newmarket, for York, on Wednesdays and Saturdays, at 6 in the morning, and arrive in York at 2 P. M. on the same days.

Price for passengers conveyed between York and Newmarket, six shillings and three pence currency, and in proportion for shorter distances. Packages carried on this route at moderate rates.

Mr. BARBER will accommodate passengers arriving with the Mail Stage at Newmarket; and they may be comfortably conveyed to the Holland Landing, or in other directions if required.

York, March 30th, 1829. 254z.

TO THE FREE AND INDEPENDENT ELECTORS OF THE TOWN OF YORK.

GENTLEMEN: I have been requested to stand forward as a Candidate for your suffrages at the approaching Election.—This request has come from those who could have been actuated by no other than public motives. I therefore take this opportunity of announcing my intention to comply with their wishes, and respectfully solicit your support.

I am, Gentlemen,
Your sincere well wisher
and Fellow Townsman,
272z. ROBERT BALDWIN.

DESIRABLE PROPERTY IN YORK TO LET.

TO LET and entry to be given immediately, that central, large and commodious dwelling house, on King Street, west of Yonge Street now occupied by the subscriber, containing eight apartments, and a kitchen—with stabling, yard, &c. The premises possess accommodations for a large family, or will answer for a dwelling house and store.

New HAT STORE YORK.

JOHN BENNETT, wishes respectfully to inform his friends and the public, that he has commenced the Hatting business, on Yonge Street, between Montgomery's and Wilmot's taverns, where he has and intends keeping on hand a general assortment of Hats and Bonnets, which he flatters himself will be of as good quality and as cheap as can be had elsewhere.

N. B. All orders received with thankfulness and attended to with punctuality.

Furs wanted.
June 19th, 1829. 255z.

CAME into the premises of the Subscriber, along with his cattle, about the first of May last, and is now in his enclosure, A RED STAG, about 3 years old, the right ear has a slit in it and a small piece cut off the left. The owner is requested to prove property, pay charges and take him away.

GEORGE GARBUTT.
Etobicoke, Lot No. 25, Con. A, Nov. 2, 1831. 83⁷p.

RED LION INN,

MARKET LANE;

Within a few rods of the Market, and directly between the two principal wharves;

YORK, UPPER CANADA.

JOHN M. WAUGH respectfully informs the Public in general, that he has taken that well known and liberally patronized Inn, recently occupied by

Mr. JOHN WILMOT,

and hopes by unremitting attention to his business, to merit a share and continuation of the patronage of a generous public.

Many *improvements* having lately been added to the House; together with the advantages of

GOOD STABLING & A CONVENIENT YARD,

must necessarily be an inducement for those to call who wish for *comfort, convenience,* and *moderate bills.* However, it is the advice of the Proprietor to call and judge for yourselves.

N. B. Baggage Stored free of Charge.
York, August 6th, 1831. 77z.

The mob, headed and urged on by their new official allies, after burning the effigy attacked the Advocate Office, smashed the windows, and destroyed some of the type; they would have laid the whole establishment in ruins had it not been for the exertions of a few active individuals. A very trusty and faithful apprentice who has been long in the office, fired off a gun loaded with powder to frighten the ruffians and protect his master's property. For having done so we learn that they have vowed to take his life, and against their cruelty and vindictiveness we are afraid we will be unable to afford him protection.

Capt. Fitzgibbon it appears was absent from the meeting; but he came down at this stage of the business, and altho' he refused to concur in Mr. Mackenzie's request to call out the military to prevent further loss of property or injury to person, he took an active and efficient part in behalf of the peace of the town, and His Excellency sent orders to the Sheriff to take every possible precaution, and held a captain's guard of soldiers ready to act at a moment's warning.

Three or four of the magistrates set up all night in the police office. Special Constables were sworn in. A voluntary guard of the towns people watched at the Advocate Office and Mr. Mackenzie's house. The former was assailed early next morning, as may be seen by our next page, and the most dreadful threats of vengeance continue to be fulminated by an ignorant and infuriated banditti who hold their nocturnal orgies at some of the taverns which the magistrates allow to be kept open at all hours of the night, and disturb the public peace in a manner which the townspeople would not tolerate for a moment if they had the means of organizing and electing an effective police. The most vile and worthless characters obtain licence; & taverns & pothouses increase to a degree that is destructive of good morals.

Extracts from the Colonial Advocate

Ads and notices (the first four from the issue of September 3, 1829, the last two from that of November 17, 1831) and part of Mackenzie's that the government had organized poverty-stricken Irishmen who were on the public dole to cause trouble for the Reform-ers.* The *Courier*, on the other hand, claimed that Mackenzie had packed the meeting with shabbily dressed farmers from his constituency.

The first conflict between the rival groups developed over the choice of chairman. The Reformers wanted Jesse Ketchum; the Tories shouted for Dr Dunlop. Sheriff Jarvis decided the matter. He had the groups vote by moving to the right or left and then counted heads. Dunlop was declared elected. James Lesslie described in his diary what happened next.

Altho' there was not less than 2/3ds of the numbers present on the liberals' side, yet did the Sheriff decide it to be on the side of the Tories. Dr D[unlop] then attempted to address the meeting but very justly was not permitted, being unfairly chosen. J. Ketchum then took the Chair in a waggon (for the Tories would not allow the other party to get access to the Chair on the Court House steps) & moved westward to prevent annoyance from them. On the chairs being taken & Mac & a few of his friends having stationed themselves beside the chairman, an attempt was made by the former to address the meeting. But no sooner was the attempt made than hooting & yelling from the Tories and their adherents pre-vented him from being heard. The utmost good humour was shown them in return; their disturbance was returned by cheers, and when all attempts to excite angry feelings were found to be in vain, the Tories tried another expedient— casting stones, rotten eggs &c. &c. at the Chairman & persons

---

* Humours of '37: "The Compact had a lot of hangers-on who would do anything that they were told for the soup, clothes, and stuff that was given them, and we used to call them 'soupets', like the bits of bread you put in soup to sop it up."

---

account of the meeting of March 23, 1832 (from the Advocate *of March 28). The Red Lion Inn advertised here is not to be confused with the inn of the same name north of York on Yonge Street.*

beside him. During all these shameful proceedings the author-
ities were among the disturbers of the peace and if they did
not aid them they did at least give them countenance. But
some say they were among the aggressors themselves. This
further outrage against the friends of Liberty excited not the
least retaliation, but all was received with the most patient
endurance. Another & brutal expedient was then resorted to.
A party of Irish Roman Catholics—evidently marshalled for
the purpose, armed with clubs—made an attack upon the
waggon & assailed indiscriminately everyone on the Liberal
side. The latter prudently & wisely yielded & withdrew aside.
The table & chairs in the waggon were shattered to pieces &
used ["by them" interpolated] as instruments of attack.
Some persons were severely injured and 1 or 2, it was feared,
had their skulls fractured—particularly Shannon, a shoe-
maker. All got out of the waggon but Mr Ketchum & away
the savages ran with it & were checked before the Court
House by running against one of the limit rails.

Finally Sheriff Jarvis was able to calm the rioters. After
the Tory group made speeches denying that the colony was
in a bad state, he proclaimed the wisdom of the government
and the crowd shouted its support for the Lieutenant-Governor. Then, standing on a chair, Mackenzie addressed the
meeting. He spoke about the blessings of the constitution,
"the corruptions which existed here, and the necessity of
manfully upholding our rights". There were cheers and jeers,
pushing and shoving.

According to Lesslie, when the Irish rowdies became forti-
fied with liquor they paraded an effigy of Mackenzie through
the streets and made an unsuccessful attack on his office. A
different account was given by the *Courier*. The effigy of
Mackenzie was hung "upon a high pole, having a large ginger-

bread cake suspended from its neck by a yellow ribbon". About 2:30 p.m. it was set on fire in front of the *Advocate* office and then the Irishmen pitched stones through an upper window in which hung a French revolutionary flag.

The *Courier* claimed that another riot almost broke out when Mackenzie and his friends made a futile attempt to drive off the attackers. "We never before witnessed", the Tory paper wrote, "so awful a transition from the pinnacle of mob favour to the lowest abyss of popular indignation and hate." The crowds that gathered were so much in opposition to Mackenzie that he hurried off to Government House and pleaded with Sir John Colborne for police protection. Fitz-Gibbon appointed special constables to guard Mackenzie and his establishment that night, but nothing further happened.

The people of turbulent York breathed a sigh of relief when Mackenzie, accompanied by his wife, left for England to present his petitions to the Colonial Office.* (The *Courier* speculated hopefully on the failure of the mission: "A man who has been twice ignominiously and deservedly expelled from the house of Assembly can never be received by a British Minister—can never be countenanced by a British Parliament." If he was received or heard, "we would not answer for the continuance of this Province as an appendage to the Empire for the space of three years.") They enjoyed the twenty-nine-day voyage from New York to Portsmouth. The long slow trip gave Mackenzie an opportunity to settle down after his Upper Canadian wars. For the first time in several years he read for pleasure; he drank and ate well and took time to compile a selection of his articles into a loosely

* Randall Wixon was put in charge of the *Colonial Advocate* while the Mackenzies were away.

organized, occasionally contradictory though genial book, which was published in London in 1833 as *Sketches of Canada and the United States.* After the intensity and hostility of recent *Colonial Advocate* columns, *Sketches* was a happy contrast.

The Mackenzies arrived in England amid the political excitement over the proposed Great Reform Bill. After centuries of aristocratic rule the British parliament under a Whig ministry had passed a bill abolishing many so-called "rotten boroughs"* and moved England towards the democratic principle of one man, one vote. Radical English parliamentarians and their supporters were pressuring the House of Lords, which was dominated by the Tory landed class, to pass the bill. Even King William threatened to create more Whig peers if the Lords did not pass the Reform Bill. The tension was such that Mackenzie wrote home to the *Colonial Advocate* that he had seen the Duke of Wellington, "the hero of Waterloo, pelted with mud and fish heads in the streets of London. Tory peers were hissed, hooted, and groaned at as they entered their carriages" after leaving the House of Lords.

The Lords passed the bill by a slim majority and Mackenzie shared in the exultation of the people. Looking back at Upper Canada he realized that under the present circumstances this great victory could not be duplicated at home. There was no way that even a Reform Assembly could force the government to make democratic changes. The councils and the Lieutenant-Governor were set in their Tory ways and would remain so—unless the British forced change upon

---

* These were rural ridings that, as a result of industrialization and the attendant migration of people to urban areas, were now sparsely populated but had equal voting power with great new manufacturing centres.

them. Mackenzie was in England to present his case for reform to the Colonial Office and ask for British intervention. This, he believed, would be forthcoming once the Colonial Office received the people's petitions and knew their true feelings. He set out to find Lord Goderich.

Sir John Colborne had anxiously written to Goderich warning him of Mackenzie's mission and asking, for the sake of colonial harmony, to pay him no heed. Why should the Colonial Office listen to a private citizen when the Lieutenant-Governor and other officials were in Upper Canada with the express purpose of keeping Britain in touch with the colony?

Mr Mackenzie has now laboured for more than seven years to create discontent in the province. He possesses that cunning and effrontery which will generally attract the attention of some part of the populace and ensure the success of any demagogue. He has had recourse to every species of falsehood and deception which would promote his views and get his journal into circulation.

Goderich, in fact, had little choice but to listen to Mackenzie because the English radicals were in their ascendancy. Mackenzie had met four of them—Joseph Hume, Francis Place, Daniel O'Connell, and William Place. (He hit it off especially well with Hume.) The Whig government found it politically expedient to respect Hume and his friends. On July 2, 1832 Mackenzie appeared before the Colonial Secretary and was received (in a face-saving gesture) as a private citizen, not as an official representative of Upper Canada. Denis Viger, the agent of the Assembly of Lower Canada, and the Reverend George Ryerson (Egerton's brother), pleading for educational reform on behalf of the Upper Canadian Methodists, were seen at the same time.

A month later Hume, Viger, and Mackenzie returned for more talks, and at a third and private meeting Goderich asked Mackenzie to put down all his complaints in writing.

Through the summer and fall of 1832 Mackenzie slaved feverishly over letters, papers, and reports, which he submitted in a stream to Goderich.* He often worked all night long by candlelight, revising his submissions until his fingers ached and his head throbbed.

His suggested reforms were wide in scope and rambled on for page after page with no apparent order of priorities. He was probably trying to show that it was in the best interests of Britain and the colony that the latter be given a large measure of self-government. The most important step in this regard was to make the Legislative Council responsible to the people—to the group holding the majority of seats in the Assembly. To reduce the Tory stranglehold on the province he advocated that control of education be withdrawn from the leadership of the Church, and that any claims for an "Established Church" be rejected by recognition of the religious pluralism of Upper Canadian society. He also requested municipal autonomy for the expanding trade and manufacturing centres that had suddenly mushroomed into towns along the shores of Lakes Ontario and Erie. Mackenzie very firmly stressed the need for commercial independence for Upper Canada and showed that Lower Canadian dominance of international trade and its administration of customs duties were detrimental to the growth of the economy.

By late fall Mackenzie was discouraged. All his work seemed to have brought no results.

The longer I remain here the more clearly I see that Whigs and Tories are neither more nor less than two parties or

* He also contributed articles to the London *Morning Chronicle*.

factions of wealthy and influential men who have conspired to plunder the great body of the people time about ... the Whigs taking the helm when the Tories become too detestable to be endured, and going below whenever Toryism has got a refreshed character by a few years' pretended opposition to misrule.

For the first time Mackenzie's high regard for the morality and supreme justice of the British government began to crack. He wondered about his future.

The Colonial Secretary was a highly competent person; he took the trouble to read Mackenzie's submissions and make notes on them. Some, he found, were "singularly ill-adapted to bring questions of so much intricacy and importance to a definite issue." Any time the Reformer overstepped his bounds, made mistakes, or exaggerated his position, Goderich took note. Replying to Mackenzie's allegations of abuse of freedom of the press, Goderich remarked: "It is needless to look beyond Mr Mackenzie's journal to be convinced that there is no latitude which the most ardent lover of free discussion ever claimed which is not at present enjoyed with perfect impunity in Upper Canada."

He agreed with Mackenzie that there were a few problems in the colonial system of government. In a dispatch sent to Colborne in November 1832 he indicated that, however acrimonious the tone of Mackenzie's charges, "I am not disposed to withdraw my attention from any useful suggestions that they may contain for the public good." He listed a number of changes he felt could be made. In reference to Mackenzie's expulsions from the Assembly, Goderich instructed Colborne "neither to practise, nor to allow ... those who are officially subordinate to you any interference with the right of his subjects to the free and unbiased choice of their representa-

tives". He advised Archdeacon Strachan and Bishop Macdonell to resign from the Legislative Council—a move that
Colborne had suggested for Strachan three years before.
Furthermore Goderich recommended that all public financial
accounts be placed before the Assembly for scrutiny. This
was a minimal response to Mackenzie's six-month-long flood
of recommendations; still, the changes were desirable from
the Reform point of view.

The dispatch did not arrive in York until early in 1833.
Colborne, who was told to make public as much of its
content as he thought convenient, was horrified that *any*
attention whatsoever had been given Mackenzie. (Even the
Lieutenant-Governor had been caught up in the animosity
and rancour that had swept the province in the past two
years.) Perhaps to spite Goderich he decided to read the
entire dispatch before the Assembly and the Legislative
Council.

The reaction was indignant. The Council refused to accept
the dispatch, much less consider its contents. The appointed
Council members deplored the fact that Goderich would
condescend to receive the disreputable Mackenzie. His charges were "outrageously insulting to all the constituted authorities of this colony and scarcely less so to the people at
large". The dispatch was returned "with the most unqualified
contempt".

Attorney-General Boulton told the Assembly that it was a
waste of time to "sit down and answer all this rigmarole
trash" and that the less publicity given to Mackenzie the
better. Solicitor-General Hagerman spoke against a motion
that the dispatch and supporting documents of Mackenzie
authorship be printed; in a vote of 21 to 12 they were
excluded from the *Journal of Proceedings*. The *Gazette* refer-

red to Goderich's communiqué as "an elegant piece of fiddle-faddle, . . . full of clever stupidity and condescending impertinence". The over-reaction of the Assembly and the Council (which were both controlled by the Tories) to a dispatch that had successfully avoided the majority of Mackenzie's complaints encouraged the Reformers to think that there must be even more corruption hidden away than they could imagine. By the same token Upper Canadians were led to believe that Mackenzie had accomplished a great deal, and the *Colonial Advocate* did nothing to disabuse them of this impression.

The Tories had waited until the expelled Mackenzie was safely in England before calling a by-election in November 1832 to fill his York County seat. To their chagrin he was re-elected *again* and they grew desperate to be rid of him. On February 9, 1833, immediately after Goderich's dispatch was expunged from the *Journals,* they once more declared Mackenzie ineligible to vote in the Assembly.

Unfortunately for the Tories the Colonial Secretary heard of the treatment they had accorded his dispatch at the same time that he was informed of their latest action against Mackenzie. In the face of such disobedience he was no longer in a mood for arguments, and in cold formal anger he wrote to Boulton: "His Majesty is interested to inform you and the Solicitor-General that His Majesty regrets he can no longer avail himself of your services and that you are to be relieved from the duties of your respective offices." In a letter of explanation to Colborne, Goderich said that both Boulton and Hagerman had "taken a part directly opposed to the avowed policy of His Majesty's Government", and as public officers, if they wished to be free "to follow the dictates of their own judgment", they must be dismissed.

Mackenzie's acceptance by the Colonial Office had been a severe blow to Tory morale, but now that two of their own clan had been disgraced, the whole system of colonial government appeared to be in jeopardy. An Assembly committee reported what many extreme Reformers had been saying for years: the colony was under the control of Britain and had to follow every whim of the Colonial Office.

We humbly submit that no law ought to be, or rightfully can be, dictated to or imposed upon the people of this province to which they do not freely give their consent through the constitutional medium of representatives chosen and accountable to themselves.

The ultra-Tory *Courier* carried the argument a step further and suggested that the future of Upper Canada perhaps lay outside the influence of Great Britain—that the people were beginning

to cast about in their mind's eye for some new state of political existence which shall effectually put the colony beyond the reach of injury and insult from any and every ignoramus whom the political lottery may chance to elevate to the chair of the Colonial Office.

The Tories had always thought of themselves as protectors of British institutions, especially the monarchy, against American republicanism. Now here was the British government treating respectfully the petitions of William Lyon Mackenzie and appearing thereby to give aid and comfort to democracy! The Tories were mortified.

4

The End of a Career

Mackenzie had reason to feel satisfied with the result of his labours. But the pleasure he took from Goderich's response to his submissions was offset by his exhaustion—at one point he had written ceaselessly for a week; by the frustration and tedium of sitting for hours on end as a suppliant, albeit a fairly successful one, in the waiting-room of the Colonial Office; and by lack of money. He had been paid only one quarter of the amount promised him for expenses by his supporters back home and had to borrow from the Reverend George Ryerson.

Isabel gave birth to a son—named Joseph Hume after the radical politician—which brightened the winter for Mackenzie. A trip to Dundee in April was eagerly anticipated, but the visit to childhood haunts and a reunion with relatives and friends were spoiled when he saw the ugliness of his birthplace, now industrialized, and the misery of workers there. Back in London his sense of accomplishment was shattered when he learned that Boulton and Hagerman had been restored to favour by E.G. Stanley, the new Colonial Secretary. Hagerman was returned to his old position of Solicitor-General and Boulton had actually been promoted: he was made Chief Justice of Newfoundland. (He was dismissed from this post in 1838 for meddling in politics.) It was the supreme double-cross. Here was incontrovertible proof that Upper Canada was ruled by the whims of the British government, a fact that even the Tory *Courier* recognized when it referred to "the lottery of British politics". Mackenzie never again fully trusted Britain.

He returned to York in late August. As if disappointment in England were not enough to bear, he found that the money promised for his journey was not forthcoming; approximately £500 remained unpaid.* The December 5 issue of the *Advocate*—the word "Colonial" had been dropped from the title for it was considered degrading—complained that $10,000 in business debts had piled up while he was fighting for the rights of the province. "I had no distrust of my own sincerity in the cause of the people," he wrote, "but I begin to distrust the people themselves."

Over the next few months, however, his York County constituents proved their trust in *him:* they re-elected him in October 1833. The Assembly expelled him in November and a by-election in York riding was held on December 16. The Assembly was in session that day and the *Patriot and Farmer's Monitor* reported that the proceedings were interrupted by a noisy flag-bearing mob that filled the gallery. Wearing his gold medal and chain, Mackenzie walked into the chamber with a statement from the York returning officer in his hand: he had been unanimously re-elected.

A heated debate ensued between Peter Perry—Bidwell's fellow Assemblyman from Lennox and Addington and a figure of growing importance in Reform ranks—and Allan

---

* A year and a half later a select committee of the Reform Assembly of 1835 was appointed to investigate the indebtedness incurred by Mackenzie's trip. It was reported that, in the interests of the province, the government should pay the £500. The political fortunes of the province, however, never allowed this payment to be made.

Napier MacNab, a former Strachan pupil, member for the Tory riding of Wentworth, and like Perry the son of a Loyalist. Perry declared that there was no legal basis for keeping Mackenzie out; MacNab argued that a proper writ had not been sent to the Assembly by the returning officer. He summed up the feelings of the majority by saying: "I sincerely trust that the house will consider its dignity and not allow themselves to be insulted by a lawless rabble, tremendous hisses, and shouting from the gallery." The Assembly voted Mackenzie out. When he resisted the sergeant-at-arms, his friends in the gallery rushed down the stairs to help him at the entrance. The legislators had the sense not to force the issue and the doors were merely barred to keep out the mob. Mackenzie stayed inside while the members carried on a two-hour debate over his case. The next day, December 17, the Assembly voted not to allow Mackenzie to take his oath of office or his seat, on the grounds that he had not made reparations for previous misconduct; the vote was 22 to 18.

The next episode of this battle of wills did not occur until February 11, 1834, when Mackenzie, after announcing his intention in the *Advocate*, made another attempt to enter the Assembly. This time he came in carrying a copy of his oath of office, which had been taken before a commissioner appointed by the Lieutenant-Governor. Mackenzie was prepared for a good fight.

The Assembly refused to back down and acknowledge Mackenzie's right to his seat. A scuffle resulted when the sergeant-at-arms was forced to remove the indomitable "firebrand" (as he was called by the Tory *Patriot*). Twice more he came back in—sneaking into the chamber, reported the hostile *Patriot*, and hiding behind desks and pillars until the watchful eye of the sergeant spotted him. The Tories were indignant. Jesse Ketchum, who was extremely popular and one of the few people who seemed to understand Mackenzie, warned his fellow members:

You have got Mr Mackenzie very low down. Take care you do not end your proceedings by raising him higher and higher in the esteem of the province. The Canadians are a generous, friendly people. They do not like to see a man persecuted. They think, and I think, your conduct towards him unfair and unlawful. He makes some very great blunders but you cover them by making still greater. Our persecution of him may end in placing him, Mr Speaker, in the chair you now fill.

When the Assembly laughed at this projection, Ketchum replied: "You may make him governor before the game is over."

Mackenzie was forceably evicted the second time, but on his third appearance the Assembly placed him in custody. He was kept in the House, but ignored by its members. The *Patriot*'s reporter was shocked by the agitated little man's features—"the peering and distorted eyeball, the blanched cheek, the uplifted wig, and the trembling limb". Mackenzie was not intimidated by his arrest. "I greatly desire personal liberty; but the fear of a prison, or of poverty, or of danger to life or limb will not, I trust, make a coward of me in a good cause." When the time came for the adjournment of the Assembly at 9:30 p.m., the Speaker admonished Mackenzie and released him from custody.

An upshot of the December 17 expulsion was a letter written to Mackenzie by Joseph Hume; it arrived in Upper Canada in May 1834. Hume stated in part that "your triumphant election . . . must hasten the crisis which is fast approaching in the affairs of Canada, and which will terminate in independence and freedom from the baneful domination of the mother country, and the tyrannical conduct of a small and despicable faction in the colony." Mackenzie fancied Hume's letter a mirror of his own thinking and published it on May 22. The reaction in town was immediate. Within six hours a petition of 1,200 names had been garnered to show the support of the population for British institutions and to express their repugnance to Hume's radical thought and his disloyal meddling in the peace and order of Upper Canada. Many people began to wonder about Mackenzie's loyalty to the existing form of British colonial government.

When Egerton Ryerson was in England in 1832 he witnessed the debate over the introduction of the Great Reform Bill and became convinced that radicals in Great Britain were attempting to destroy parliamentary government. For all his dislike of the Tory establishment of Upper Canada, Ryerson was a British loyalist, anti-American, and hostile to republicanism. When he came back to Canada he spoke out against the alliance that Mackenzie had made with British radicalism and his friendship with Joseph Hume. Ryerson was the editor of the Methodist *Christian Guardian,* which had the largest newspaper circulation in the province, and his views were well known and respected. Many Methodists were impressed with Ryerson's apparent change of allegiance.

Mackenzie was furious. It was *his* newspaper that had first publicized Ryerson. He wrote in the *Advocate* that Ryerson "has gone over to the enemy, press, types, and all, and hoisted the colours of a cruel, vindictive tory priesthood." Even Joseph Hume joined in, declaring from England that he had never known "a more worthless hypocrite or so base a man as Mr Ryerson has proved himself to be". In this era, if a

Toronto, 1835, from the south side of King Street, showing the jail with the stocks in front, the Fireman's Hall facing Church Street (designed by the artist, John Howard). No figures were

Toronto, 1835, looking east along King Street from

man changed his politics or religion he was considered a traitor for the rest of his life by many of his former compatriots. Mackenzie, who could tolerate only those who accepted his methods and ideas, now put Ryerson on his blacklist along with Strachan and Robinson.

In the ten years of Mackenzie's residence in York—from 1824 to 1834—the population had grown by 550 per cent, from 1,685 to 9,252. Increase in numbers had brought some benefits, but to the casual observer the contrast between rich and poor was the most evident change. A St Catharines newspaper in the summer of 1833 mockingly compared American towns to York, where an overburdensome bureaucracy was found living amidst ugly and wretched surroundings.

It is truly humbling to the proud spirit of a British subject to . . . look at York—the capital of the Province, the seat of government, the residence of His Majesty's representative and my Lord Chief Justice, of the honourable and reverend, and honourables without reverend, with all the sub-honourables and dishonourables, judges, councillors, barristers, attorneys, magistrates, sheriffs, bailiffs and jailors—York, the senior some twenty years of Rochester or Buffalo . . . containing in its very centre old dilapidated white-washed log cottages, stables, cow yards, pig styes, and out-houses next to the street, and dwellings in the rear; foul and disgusting lanes and alleys, filthy gutters, and muddy unpaved streets.

Poverty-stricken immigrants often moved into already crowded parts of town, some of which had a reputation for vice. Teraulay Street was known for its alcoholics and Lombard Street for prostitution. Francis Collins wrote a scathing article denouncing those who aided and abetted the degradation of women.

Houses of infamy are scattered thro' every corner of the town ... and one of them had the hardihood to commence operations next door to our office last week, in a house under the control of a police magistrate. ... So besotted are some of our would-be gentlemen ... that they crowded to it at noonday, and some of them that we know visited it in open day last Sabbath!

Formerly York was plagued with conflicts between youths of the "old" and "new" towns. Now there were political street fights—such as the one that occurred on March 23, 1832—abetted by unemployed Irish immigrants and rowdy farm boys in town for adventure. Better police protection was only one reason why for several years leading citizens had been advocating the incorporation of York as a city. The single member for York in the provincial Assembly was unable to interest rural members in urban problems, and revenue was not readily available for special town needs. The merchants and traders wanted a local government and a moderate tax levy for capital improvements on streets and buildings that would promote the economic and commercial advancement of the community. The Reformers were quick to see incorporation as a means of limiting government patronage, for the city could then take over the appointment of the magistrates from the Lieutenant-Governor.

It was proposed that the city government be made up of a mayor, and two aldermen and two councillors from each of five wards.* The mayor was to be elected by this group from among themselves. Also proposed in the incorporation was a change of name, for the inhabitants were irritated that their town was called *Muddy Little* York. The Assembly of 1834

* St David, St George, St Patrick, St Andrew, and St Lawrence (for Canada)—names that reflected the ethnic background of the city's inhabitants.

considered a few names but the choice narrowed down to "York" and the aboriginal name "Toronto" (meaning the "meeting place" of Indian tribes). The Speaker, Archibald McLean, thought that the name Toronto was "pleasing to the ear" and somewhat "musical". Bidwell, the ex-Speaker, "wished the present name retained—Toronto for poets, York for men of business". Some Tories wanted to keep the royal name of York for sentimental reasons. William Dummer Powell, the retired Chief Justice, referred ambiguously to "the wild and Terrific Sound of TORONTO". Finally the town of York was incorporated as the city of Toronto on March 6, 1834.

Undaunted by his expulsions from the Assembly, Mackenzie became a candidate for alderman and let it be known that he would make a fine mayor. When the city elections were held on March 27, 1834, the five wards gave Reform-minded candidates the majority of seats (12 to 8). The new aldermen and councillors in turn elected Mackenzie, alderman from St David's ward, as their first mayor. On March 28 the *Patriot*, which had recoiled in horror when Mackenzie announced his candidacy, did not attempt to hide its disappointment with the election results but optimistically expressed the hope that the politicians would see to "draining, paving or McAdamizing the streets and flagging the sidewalks".

Between April 8 and June 19 rules for the city council were established, committees were set up, offices were opened in the market building (which became known as the City Hall), and nine bylaws were passed. But almost nothing of a constructive nature was accomplished by the council thereafter. Even allowing for the inexperience of Mackenzie and his councillors, his brief term of office (with a Reform majority) did very little for the city and revealed no hidden gifts in Mackenzie as a leader. There was much wrangling at council meetings between Tories and Reformers, particularly over appointments and taxes. The financial problems of the city went from bad to worse and no policy was established— Mackenzie never had a very firm grasp of money matters. It soon became clear that he was not able to focus on one job exclusively and do it well. In May he was distracted by the trouble over the Hume letter and by July he was preparing to run in the provincial election. As mayor, Mackenzie acted as presiding magistrate and inevitably aroused criticism for his sentences—notably when Ellen Halfpenny, who had been brought before him on a charge of drunken and disorderly conduct, was sentenced to the stocks. She had thrown a shoe at him after he reprimanded her for shouting abuse.

Mackenzie conscientiously attempted to have the city's sidewalks and roads improved, but higher taxes necessary to pay for such work brought howls of indignation. In a body the Tories on city council consistently voted against raising taxes, and Mackenzie—by his own published statements ideologically opposed to high taxes—was forced to champion the Reform council's tax measures in the city. (The taxation issue revolved specifically around a sidewalk of four twelve-inch planks placed side by side and laid lengthways on each side of King Street at a cost of £1,000.) Some citizens tried to organize a movement to refuse to pay any taxes on the grounds that they had been unfairly assessed.

Frustrated with the obstructive tactics of Tories on the council, and alarmed by the adverse public response, Mackenzie went over the head of the elected city government and called a public meeting to explain the problem and arouse support. The gathering was called for July 29 at 5 p.m. when, according to the *Patriot,* street workers and labourers (who

Isabel Mackenzie, 1834

William Lyon Mackenzie, 1834, painted after he became mayor.

did not have property and did not pay municipal taxes) would be off work and could bolster up their boss, the mayor.

The meeting turned into a shouting match between Mackenzie and Toronto Assemblyman Sheriff Jarvis, each disclaiming the authority of the other to address the gathering. Both men had groups of supporters to back them. Charles Lindsey relates that when Mackenzie could finally be heard he explained the assessment, the nature of the roads, the money needed to keep them in repair, the previous city debt, and the £9,400 still outstanding for the new brick market building with its auditorium, in which they were meeting. The *Patriot* reported on the same speech but merely said in the exaggerated journalistic language of the day that Mackenzie ranted and raved for over an hour against persons connected with the government and those who were fortunate in business.

The rival groups shouted, hissed, and screamed, and the meeting broke up in disorder. A second was called for the next day in the market square, where there was a balcony for spectators. A large crowd gathered here and peered down on the assembled mob. Jarvis again tore into the mayor's policies. He was reported to have said: "I care no more for Mackenzie than"—he looked up at a crow flying overhead—"that crow!" The crowd, in appreciation of his oratory, cheered and stamped their feet. The vibrations loosened a portion of the balcony and down it fell, people and all.

The victims screamed in anguish. Their falling bodies, wrote the *Patriot,* "produced an instantaneous scene of unequalled horror"; some were impaled on butcher hooks hanging in the stalls below the balcony, others broke limbs, or suffered internal injuries or skin lacerations. Among the five dead was the sixteen-year-old son of James FitzGibbon. The *Courier,* whose editor George Gurnett was hurt in the disaster, indignantly reported on the reaction of Mackenzie's supporters to the plight of the unfortunate—most of whom apparently were Tories.

There was nothing half so horrid, not even the mangled bodies of the dead and dying, as the vociferous yell of triumph which a party of Mr Mackenzie's adherents . . . set up when they saw those mangled bodies laying before them, a yell which they accompanied with clapping of hands, waving of hats, and with the exclamation of "There go the d—d Tories!" and "The d—d Tories are down now!"

Mackenzie, who had not yet arrived at the market when the calamity occurred, was mainly concerned with the unfavourable public response to the incident. Some people accused him of being responsible for what happened because he should never have called the first meeting. The *Advocate* claimed the Tories were looking for revenge.

We are credibly informed that Mr Samuel Peters Jarvis, who headed the press riot, asked the other day whether a party could not be collected to murder Mr Mackenzie. Such is the state of society in Toronto.

In the summer of 1834 another disaster hit York—cholera. The dread disease was brought to the province by immigrants, most of whom were poor and unprepared physically and materially for the long ocean voyage to America. Many died enroute in the dark, dirty, crowded holds of vessels where the cholera spread. Those who arrived safely soon communicated the disease to people in Quebec, Montreal, and Toronto.

According to Charles Lindsey, Mackenzie helped as much as he could, taking victims by cart from their homes to the ill-equipped and overcrowded hospital. Pushing himself to the utmost of his endurance, Mackenzie came down with a mild form of the disease himself; he was fortunate to recover with no after-effects.

As a result of the epidemic, citizens became more conscious of the need for sanitation. The community undertook to clean and wash all houses with lime, drain many low-lying areas, water the dusty streets, and burn tar, pitch, and sulphur every day in the hope that the "diseased air" would be purified. When it was noticed that alcoholics seemed to be particularly susceptible to cholera, zealous magistrates had all the drunkards found on the streets rounded up and put in jail or the stocks to keep them away from the bottle.

The swelling population of Toronto brought not only disease but a growing sophistication and interest in culture and adult education. The upper class had a Literary and Philosophical Society. For the growing middle class of tradesmen and small shopkeepers there was a "Mechanics' Institute".* To the old small-town pastimes—"subscription balls, whist, unorganized sport and incessant visiting"—and the inevitable tavern life were added amateur theatricals, circuses, travelling showmen, puppet shows, concerts, lectures and "exhibitions ranging from a wax figure of 'Duncan Bradley, the Yorkshire giant' and Easby the Perth murderer's skin, to subjects of wider local interest such as the Grand Panoramic View of Bytown and the fattest heifer in Upper Canada", as well as plays by American touring companies.

Mackenzie did not appreciate the theatre and thought it a bad influence on the community. The fact that plays were held in taverns and strolling players were of questionable character made it all the worse. Mackenzie was also disgusted

* On July 1, 1883 it was taken over by the Toronto Public Library.

with the amount of drinking done in town and the resulting inebriation. A new trend was started: Methodists and some political Reformers, John Rolph and Jesse Ketchum among them, made an attempt to curb drinking by promoting temperance societies. They were not very successful and the Tory *Patriot* dubbed their members as "old men and maidens, widows and wives". Colonel Talbot, a renowned bachelor and land dealer, of Irish descent, called them "damn cold-water drinking societies".

Mackenzie was mayor of Toronto for only nine months. Already dispirited by the market catastrophe and the cholera epidemic, the populace turned against the first municipal government because of its high taxes and lack of achievement; the Tory aldermen were looked upon with particular favour because they had opposed the tax increases. It was left to Mackenzie's successors to provide the leadership and the improvements the city so badly needed.*

While he was still mayor, Mackenzie resolved to run again for a York County seat in the provincial election in the fall of 1834. As usual he began a vicious journalistic campaign. He published an almanack under one of his old pseudonyms, Patrick Swift ("Professor of Astrology")—after the satirist Jonathan Swift. It was a propaganda piece entitled *A New Almanack for the Canadian True Blues . . . for the Millenial and prophetical year of the Grand General Election for Upper Canada, and total and everlasting downfall of Toryism in the British Empire, 1834.*

Mackenzie was becoming increasingly frustrated by his inability to change the course of Upper Canadian government through hard work and writing. The *Almanack's* epigraph

---

* Robert Baldwin Sullivan, cousin and brother-in-law of Robert Baldwin, became mayor in 1835. Mackenzie ran for alderman but was defeated.

showed the militant trend of his thinking: "If there had been no display of physical force, or public opinion, I very well know that there would have been no reform bill.—*Hume*" Among charts of the rising and setting of the sun, lists of important dates in the evolution of democracy, announcements of upcoming events, and descriptions of various provincial organizations, Mackenzie interspersed accusations, invective, and his latest ideas on governmental reform. Of the Church of England clergy, he wrote that "they may be taken by all Reformers to be political agents, spies or policemen of the Tory government". He also attacked the Methodists and Roman Catholic Bishop Macdonell for accepting government funds. In contrast to the early days of the *Colonial Advocate,* when it had supported government taxation for canals and harbours to benefit commerce, Mackenzie now proclaimed that the taxes extracted from poor farmers were used merely to bribe voters. He advocated cheap government and low taxes.

Fortunately for Mackenzie the election was not held until October 1834 when the cholera was gone, the furor over Hume's letter had died down, and the bitter argument with Ryerson partially forgotten. Opportunistically he buried his feelings about Upper Canadian independence and Britain's "baneful domination" and joined with the Reformers to persuade farmers that under a Tory Assembly they had been neglected. To work with Britain toward economic and political changes was the theme of their campaign and in those not-too-prosperous days it appealed to the rural voters. The rapid growth of population was a boon to Mackenzie in two ways: his York constituency was now divided in half (there were 4 York ridings instead of 2), leaving a much smaller area to canvass, and the new settlers had not yet experienced a

Reform Assembly and for the first time were open to his persuasive ways.

The election was almost a clean sweep for the Reformers. Many new Reform names appeared on the Assembly list: Samuel Lount from Simcoe, and from York riding David Gibson, Dr T.D. Morrison (to replace a retired Jesse Ketchum), and John Macintosh (who was married to Mackenzie's sister-in-law). Mackenzie was the fourth member for York. In Toronto Sheriff Jarvis lost to Reformer James Small—260 votes to 252. Jarvis, as the sitting member for the city riding, was blamed for the act of incorporation and for Toronto's poor municipal government—unfairly, considering the Reformers' control of city council.

Mackenzie won his seat by a wide margin and this time the Tories did not challenge his right to take his place in the Assembly. They did not have the majority of seats, of course, but in any case the previous expulsions applied only to the life of the old Assembly.

Political and economic reforms were now the sole ambition in Mackenzie's life. He abruptly decided to stop publication of the *Advocate* and people speculated about his reasons. Was Mackenzie too busy as mayor and M.P.P.? Was he in financial distress? Was there too much Reform and liberal-minded competition in the province? Or—the most likely reason—was he depressed following the death of his son Joseph Hume on October 26? The last issue came off the press on November 4, 1834. Early in 1835 the *Advocate* was incorporated with the *Correspondent,* a paper published by a former Roman Catholic priest, William O'Grady, who had fallen out with his Tory bishop, the Highland Scot Macdonell. O'Grady and Mackenzie were kindred spirits in their distaste for ecclesiastical authority, Tory politics, and British management of the colony. People could count on the *Correspondent and Advocate,* which published articles and letters by Mackenzie, to be as irritating a paper as the *Advocate.*

On December 9, 1834 Mackenzie and James Lesslie formed the Canadian Alliance Society, which was to be a clearing-house for information that would help promote change. Mackenzie wrote to a Brockville reformer, A.N. Buell, that hoped-for changes in government would be thwarted unless the population was organized. "If we enlist the people in our cause," he said, "we are safe." The lengthy reformist program of the Society included low taxes and a general retrenchment to prevent over-expansion of the economy, the "diffusion of sound political information by pamphlets and tracts", and "a close alliance with any similar association that may be formed in Lower Canada". Besides Mackenzie, the only prominent Reformers who appeared interested were Dr T.D. Morrison and William O'Grady; nevertheless there seem to have been numerous chapters around the countryside, which were formed after the initial appeal—though no activities are recorded. In any case Mackenzie's attention very quickly switched to his work in the Assembly.

The House met in January 1835. As was his custom at the opening of every session, Mackenzie gave notice of the matters he expected to be dealt with. He wanted a standing committee on currency, financial statements from banks and the Welland Canal, inquiries into the expenses of the Legislative Council, and various investigations relating to his expulsions, including publication of correspondence between the Colonial Office and the Lieutenant-Governor. A few days later he moved the formation of a standing committee on currency (of which he would be the chairman). It was roundly defeated, 47 to 2, proving that on financial and

economic matters he had lost the confidence of his former
Reform friends. The Assembly was quite willing to let him
attack the political establishment, but the members believed
in the present economic system and wanted it to expand
under government control.

On January 23 the Assembly gave Mackenzie the chair-
manship of the Select Committee on Grievances, thus allowing him to climax years of fact-collecting and anti-establish-
ment outrage by producing a document that had the power
of government and the constitution behind it. All the problems that Mackenzie had been denouncing for years could
now be brought together; his fact-filled brain and all his lists,
statistics, interviews, correspondence, and resolutions could
be put to effective use. When he called twenty-three witnesses before his Committee, embarrassing his enemies with
pointed questions and eliciting whenever possible from his
friends evidence of unfairness and injustice, he was in complete control of the proceedings and enjoyed every minute of
them.

From February 5 to April 10 there appeared before the
fierce-eyed chairman, one by one, government officials, members of the House and Councils, clergy, prominent bureau-
crats, wealthy businessmen, and ordinary citizens. Mackenzie
lectured, accused, and cajoled. Methodically he sought out
corruption; unnervingly he pounced on weaknesses and inaccuracies in the replies he was given; smoothly he encouraged
damaging complaints against the government. The Tories who
appeared before him were often contemptuously uninform-
ative or evasive in their replies. They were asked about
everything from the sources of their income to their opinions
on the established church, elections, education, and responsible government.

When fifty-seven-year-old John Strachan, the Archdeacon

of Toronto, was called to testify—his political power lessened since Maitland left the province—he remained cool and indifferent to his adversary. Mackenzie was not a credible political figure to Strachan, who referred to him dismissively as "the printer". For the greater part of the encounter Strachan refused to be upset by Mackenzie's inquiries and gave simple non-committal answers or pretended not to understand the point of the question. But Mackenzie received a firm answer when he said: "The vote by ballot in elections is prayed for in many petitions to the Assembly and to His Majesty. What is your opinion of this mode of voting?" Strachan replied: "Nobody would ask for the vote by ballot but from gross ignorance. It is the most corrupt way of using the franchise!"

William O'Grady, the former priest, testified that Bishop Macdonell preached sermons with "a strange and incoherent medley of politics and Christianity" and, "instead of preaching the morality of the Gospel", inveighed against Mackenzie "in the most violent and unbecoming manner". Mackenzie was disgusted by the close relationship between the churches and the state and he must have been pleased when O'Grady said that he could prove "unequivocally", by virtue of his former trusted place in the Roman Catholic diocese, that "His Majesty's bounty"—grants from the Colonial Office to the Church—had "been most shamefully abused". The Bishop was accused of misapplying the funds by favouring some of his clergy, and the impression was given that he may have kept a large amount for himself. Macdonell was not called to give his side of the story.

The *Seventh Report from the Select Committee of the House of Assembly of Upper Canada on Grievances* ran to over 500 printed pages (the index alone was 76 pages) and was the most detailed document that had ever been produced on the condition of Upper Canada. Mackenzie clearly stated for the first time that the province should be set adrift from the control of the Colonial Office. Under the present system, he charged, governorships were simply a matter of thoughtless British patronage (Colborne was paid £5,631 yearly; his private secretary £808) and the Lieutenant-Governor in turn appointed the two Councils on the same basis. Finally, and most discreditably, he pointed out that there were many members of the Councils who could not be considered independent because they held government jobs. The patronage system meant that orders from the Colonial Secretary and the Lieutenant-Governor were obeyed without question. The assembly, the representative branch of the colonial legislature, was powerless and therefore sorely discontented. The Committee recommended that an elected Legislative Council might be a solution to the current frustration of the people, but the *Report* was pessimistic about British rule in Upper Canada. "The whole system has so long continued virtually in the same hands that it is little better than a family compact."*

Two thousand copies of the *Report* were printed that summer by order of the Assembly, which did not adopt it when it finally appeared. An impression was conveyed that many Reformers had been more anxious to keep Mackenzie's energies focussed on the Committee than to consider seriously his suggestions and schemes. However a copy was sent to Lord Glenelg, the Colonial Secretary. The *Report* was a potential source of trouble for the British government— especially if the strong radical parliamentary opposition

---

* The term "family compact" to describe Tory government leaders was first used in 1824 by Thomas Dalton, the editor of the *Patriot*. It was later made popular by historians, but Mackenzie and other Reformers used it only occasionally.

sought to pursue the suggestion of improper colonial rule—
and Glenelg had to make a show of responding to it positive-
ly. Lieutenant-Governor Colborne was removed.*

The choice of the man who was to solve Upper Canadian
problems was typical of the "lottery system" that exem-
plified British politics. Sir Francis Bond Head was hardly
known in upper-class British circles, though the family name
was familiar to many. At the time of his appointment he was
an undistinguished Assistant Poor Law Commissioner in Kent
and had gained some prominence as the author of several
exciting books based on his cowboy experiences on the
Argentine pampas (for which he was known as "Galloping
Head"). For years after 1837 stories were told that Sir
Francis had been appointed to the position mistakenly and
that his more distinguished brother, or his cousin, was intended for the honour. Whether or not this was true, to British
authorities any "name" should be able to handle the problems of Upper Canada. In Sir Francis Bond Head the Colonial
Office had a man of integrity, courage, and devotion to duty,
but he was without an ounce of political experience and
completely lacked statesmanship. He carried out his task with
steadfast earnestness but was entirely unable to compromise;
and it was this inability that brought him into conflict with
Mackenzie—another man who did not know when to back
down.

British parliamentary reformers heard of Head's position as
Poor Law Commissioner and assumed that he was in favour
of democracy. When Head arrived in Toronto in January
1836 this reputation had preceded him and he was met with
placards and banners proclaiming him "A Tried Reformer".
Head had dutifully carried with him from England a blue-

* He was not demoted but made Governor of Lower Canada.

Sir Francis Bond Head

bound copy of the grievances report and was anxious to begin work. When he called prominent politicians to appear before him and present their cases, he soon realized that the Tories regarded him as their enemy; but "whether the Tories liked the medicine or whether they did not, I cared not a single straw." What astonished the Lieutenant-Governor was not that the Tories resisted his ministry but that the Reformers, when they were given an audience, did not care to discuss the grievances. Of Bidwell, Head wrote later: *"Never could I get him to look at the book of grievances."* Perhaps the chairman of the committee, William Lyon Mackenzie, would give him more satisfaction.

Head was a short handsome man with a dynamic personality that more than made up for his lack of height. When seated he was unable to touch the floor with his feet because of the shortness of his thighs. But his legs were never allowed to dangle; they "were thrust out stiffly in front and kept in that position, apparently without effort". An unknown witness who saw Head waiting for Little Mac was impressed with Head's posture and with some foresight remarked that he "is a man of determination and will gain his point".

When he arrived for his audience Mackenzie, also endowed with short legs, was more tense and nervous than usual. Head seems to have despised him from their first encounter.

Afraid to look me in the face, he sat, with his feet not reaching the ground and with his countenance averted from me, at an angle of about 70 degrees; while, with the eccentricity, the volubility, and indeed the appearance of a madman, the tiny creature raved in all directions.

Head could not understand why Mackenzie would not discuss the *Report.* "Sir, let us cure what we have got here first," he said. But Mackenzie was too wound up to do anything but chatter about other problems. "Nothing that I could say would induce the peddlar to face his own report."

The hoped-for constructive relationship between the Reformers and Head was doomed from the outset. The Lieutenant-Governor had expected a coherent and organized opposition party to expound its point of view in British style; instead he found a divided group. Certainly the most outspoken of their number, William Lyon Mackenzie, could not be considered a leader. His personality made him totally unfit for the give-and-take of public office. "When a practical question was put before him for a practical answer," Head noted, "the man was utterly at sea; his faculty of constructiveness was obliterated." In fact it was apparent to Head that the most respected Reformers were out of sympathy with the man who was responsible for the removal of Sir John Colborne.

Head decided in February to alter the structure of the Executive Council to make it more representative of political groupings in the province. After much persuasion Robert Baldwin, John Rolph, and John Dunn (the Receiver-General) agreed to serve as members—more to show their willingness to co-operate with the Lieutenant-Governor than with any hope that the Executive would succeed in changing government policy.

Tories, Reformers, and many who had no particular allegiance were very confused. The Lieutenant-Governor kept saying that he was neutral in political matters and was searching for the best solution to problems, but from their past experience with government the people found this hard to believe. In her journal of March 10, 1836 Mary O'Brien expressed a Tory view:

Sir John Colborne was as little a man of party as could well be ... but this man, coming out with the character of a radical, sent by a whig ministry to redress supposed grievances, and shoving into his council some of the leaders of the radical party, declares himself so unflinchingly both willing and obliged to support the constitution, and tells them in such plain terms that he must stick to the present business of the country instead of listening to bygone mismanagement ... that they are ... much puzzled by him.

In the past the Executive Council had often borne the brunt of Assembly abuse for policies created entirely by the Colonial Office and the Lieutenant-Governor. Baldwin wanted the province to know who actually made policy—because it wasn't the Council! In early March he convinced the other Council members that the time had come to ask Head to consult them on all general matters relating to the conduct of government, and that if he was not prepared to make this pledge then the people should be informed. Glenelg had insisted that the governmental system should not be altered and Head outrightly refused their proposal. He did offer to consult them when he deemed it necessary, but not about issues *they* considered important. Tories and Reformers united in a desire for more voice in their own government; all six councillors resigned.

Head immediately restructured a more conservative council, while the Reformers organized petitions and demonstrations to protest the failure of conciliatory action and co-operation. A committee chaired by Peter Perry, now obviously the leader of Assembly Reformers, investigated and reported on the resignations. The result was a highly emotional outburst against Head who, they said, conducted "our affairs" according to his own "arbitrary and vindictive" will and pleasure. The Assembly, on the advice of the committee, refused to vote any money to keep up the day-to-day expenses of government. In their defence the Assemblymen petitioned the British House of Commons and set out their point of view.

We entertain a fear, grounded on the experience of the past, that His Majesty's ear will be so abused by secret dispatches and personal detractions as almost to set at defiance the best-directed intentions of His Majesty to arrive at the truth.

Four days later, on April 19, the Speaker of the Assembly, Marshall Spring Bidwell, allowed to be read into the record a letter from Joseph Papineau, the Lower Canadian radical and future rebel leader. In this missive Papineau attacked British governing authorities and suggested that "the state of society all over continental America requires that the forms of its Government should approximate nearer to that selected . . . by the wise statesmen of the neighbouring Union than to that in which chance and past ages have moulded European societies."

Sir Francis was not to be outdone by radicals. At the end of the Assembly session he gave a lengthy summation of his policies. He castigated the members for caring more about past grievances than for future good government and prosperity. He was insulted that the Assembly should demand an accounting for what he called the "firing" of his own council. He saw their action of refusing to vote government money as a direct attack on the British monarchy. "I can give them no surer proof of my desire to preserve *their* privileges inviolate than by proving to them that I am equally determined to maintain the rights and prerogatives of *the Crown.*"

Head was a man of action. Within a month the disobedient

Assembly was dissolved and an election called. Head appealed directly to the British settlers and never varied his platform. The electors had to choose between him and the Reformers (or republicans, as he characterized them).

The Reformers were more divided than ever before. There were not sufficient votes to be obtained by opposing the government, as in previous elections, because Head had made the issue very simple: either vote for him or against Great Britain. (In his enthusiasm he had Government House painted a "loyal British Orange".) Reformers were left to fight on the strength of their individual personalities and past performance. Mary O'Brien had complained that in previous campaigns apathy in her York riding was the reason Mackenzie was consistently able to win. In a letter written at the time of the 1836 contest she stated that "the late events have roused those who before were quiet and indifferent, simply from being unoppressed and prosperous, to show themselves".

In the election, which took place from mid-June to early July, the Reformers met with disaster. Down went Bidwell and Perry in Lennox and Addington, Samuel Lount in Simcoe—and, for the first time in his provincial career, William Lyon Mackenzie in York County. In the most radical constituency in Upper Canada, Little Mac lost out to a professed moderate and political nonentity (Edward Thompson) by one hundred votes.

5

The Siege of Toronto

Mackenzie's defeat in 1836 played havoc with both his morale and his health. The effects were not immediately obvious, however. With typical resilience he began to publish another newspaper, the *Constitution,* on July 4. Its columns were not didactic, as his previous papers had been, but were filled with bitter accounts of every known discontent in the province. A pervasive theme was frustration with the British colonial system and praise of the society that existed under the government to the south.

Although humiliated by his poor showing at the polls, Mackenzie did not give up politics. He challenged the Assembly to overturn the York County election results because of irregularities in the voting procedure and spent much of the fall of 1836 trying to get evidence to support this charge. In November, taut with nervous strain, he became ill with a severe case of pleurisy; his efforts to produce a case for the Assembly were therefore seriously hampered. He presented a petition on December 20 but let the fourteen-day deadline for submission of evidence pass. The Assemblymen gladly threw it out on this technicality.

Although the Tories dominated the new Assembly, they must have been aware that their popularity, bought with the price of Head's intervention and vigorous campaigning, was

transitory and would quickly fade. The advanced age of
William IV and his reported poor health made his death and
the dissolution of the Assembly an imminent possibility. The
Tories were skeptical of their chances to make a strong
showing in another election and early in the session of 1837
passed an act that would prevent the Assembly's dissolution
in the event of the king's death.* Mackenzie was in despair
over this cunning and cavalier move. "They tremble and
shake for fear of the just retribution their covetousness has
provoked," he wrote bitterly of the Tories, "and at Head's
nod vote themselves fit to outlive kings and emperors, though
utterly unfit to face their injured country."

The whole English-speaking world was entering an economic depression that would last well into 1837. In Upper
Canada the Tory Assembly attempted to stimulate the province's economy by borrowing millions of dollars to build
railways, roads, and canals. When British investors tightened
their purse strings and withdrew money from the province,
Canadian communities ran short of cash and the government
was unable to raise funds to meet its debts. The Bank of
Upper Canada pleaded in vain with the Lieutenant-Governor
for a check on government spending and for restrictions on
the use of paper currency in a time of crisis and fiscal
insecurity. At a special session of the Assembly called in
mid-June, legislation was passed to help the banks bear up
under growing public fear that they would go bankrupt—that
paper currency would be worthless and deposits would be
lost.

Mackenzie had already made his opposition to banking
well known. In his opinion the close alliance of government
and Tory bankers had influenced elections, corrupted elected

* He was succeeded by Queen Victoria in June 1837.

representatives, tempted the farmer to bank his money rather than lend it to a worthy neighbour, and "supported every judicial villainy and oppression with which our country has been afflicted". He had also claimed that the banks encouraged the government to spend beyond its means and to tax farmers for projects that benefited only the people of Toronto.

Mackenzie became obsessed with the idea of revenging his defeat in York County by destroying those who had brought it about. He jumped at the opportunity offered by the banking crisis to bring down Head and the whole government system. "Farmers of Upper Canada", he wrote excitedly, "EXCHANGE YOUR BANK NOTES FOR GOLD AND SILVER." He hoped that a run on the banks would ruin them and purge "the nation of vile cheating bank folks". The banks, however, managed to stave off collapse even when many responded to this call.

Meanwhile events in Lower Canada were developing in such a way as to reinforce despair in the British colonial system. In a vain attempt to force the British government to make the appointed councils responsible to the group holding the majority of seats in the Assembly, the Assembly of Lower Canada had consistently refused to vote money for public expenditures. The British government became concerned and sent Lord Gosford to Lower Canada to study the situation. The resulting Ten Resolutions, which were published in Britain in 1837, not only determined the maintenance of the status quo in the colony but enabled the governor to appropriate funds that the Assembly had previously refused to sanction. Lower Canada Reformers openly advocated rebellion as their only recourse in the face of British intransigence. Mackenzie's response to the Resolutions was contained in a letter he wrote in April 1837 to Wolfred Nelson, a militant Lower Canadian.* He suggested a boycott of manufactured goods from Britain. With the current depression the Tory merchants of Canada would be strangled by an all-out public campaign against them and their British wholesalers.

In the July 5 *Constitution* Mackenzie's thoughts took a radical turn. His paper openly reviewed the possibilities of revolt in Lower Canada—of which he clearly approved—and the chances for its success. A recent visit to New York to purchase several thousand books had further strengthened his appreciation of the American way of life (as he observed it on the surface). Now that the British had proved themselves unresponsive to Lower Canadians, he decided that the obvious solution to the province's problems was an alliance with Americans, some of whom were biding their time to come and help the democratic cause in the lower province.

Over the years Mackenzie's readers had become used to his extreme and radical statements, made on the spur of the moment and often contradicted in the very next issue. The Tories therefore paid little attention to his latest tirades and failed to perceive a subtle change behind his ravings. "I am proud of my descent from a rebel race . . . this rebel blood of mine will always be uppermost," he wrote. In speaking to groups of Reformers he enumerated all the old grievances. Appointments to public office were still being given to Tories; Reformers were being persecuted (Dr Baldwin, James Small, and George Ridout had been removed from judicial and militia posts by Head for appearing at a meeting of the very moderate Constitutional Reform Society); the appoin-

*For several years Mackenzie had also been corresponding with Louis-Joseph Papineau and John Neilson, two other Lower Canadian radicals.

ted councils were reactionary and did not represent reform; the Assembly elections were engineered by the Lieutenant-Governor (as the people were only now becoming aware)—and the Assembly would be in office for four more years! Could true patriots wait that long for justice?

At public meetings held in the early summer, Mackenzie and some dissatisfied country friends, among them Samuel Lount and Silas Fletcher, slowly began to convince themselves that rebellion was sometimes a just course of action. The seeds were sown. Violence was now openly discussed as an alternative to constitutional change.

Words gave way to planned actions. On the nights of July 28 and 31, in John Doel's brewery at Bay and Adelaide Streets, Mackenzie met with Torontonians he thought might support him in promoting radical change. On a motion introduced by Mackenzie, the men pledged that they would share the fate of Lower Canada in whatever course was taken there. A Committee of Vigilance* was formed, with Mackenzie in his usual commanding position as agent and corresponding secretary. The committee was charged to seek ways of implementing united action with the lower province and to organize reform unions. A declaration to this effect, modelled on the American Declaration of Independence, was written by Mackenzie and O'Grady and published in the *Constitution* and the *Correspondent and Advocate* on August 2, 1837. The same month, pent-up with zeal, Mackenzie began a series of meetings in York County and the adjoining territory to form vigilance groups, to pass resolutions against the government, and to encourage militancy. He had been doing this on his own for several months, but now he had the approval of

* Among its members were Dr Morrison, David Gibson, John Macintosh, William O'Grady, John Montgomery, and John Doel.

some recognized and respected Reformers—though the Baldwins, Perry, Bidwell, and Rolph had not joined his organization. (Only the latter two had been asked.)

As Mackenzie proclaimed his grievances to audiences throughout the countryside, his emotions got the better of him and ideas of rebellion and a popular uprising, which had been churning at the back of his mind, at last found tongue. In Caledon a resolution was passed that said in part:

When a government is engaged in systematically oppressing a people . . . it commits the same species of wrong to them that warrants an appeal to force against a foreign enemy . . . . The glorious revolutions of 1688 on one continent and of 1776 on another may serve to remind those rulers . . . that they are placing themselves in a state of hostility against the governed; and that to prolong a state of irresponsibility and insecurity . . . is a dangerous act of aggression against a people. A magistrate who degenerates into a systematic oppressor, and shuts the gates of justice on the public, thereby restores them to their original right of defending themselves.

There were always hotheads and young bloods, anxious for a fight, who egged him on. But the majority of the rural people remained calm. Mackenzie obviously cared for them and wanted to help them, but they all knew he was belligerent, frantic, and unstable. They were cool to his anti-British statements (which he had deliberately played down) and his support for Lower Canadian Reformers (who were largely French and Roman Catholic). On the other hand the Tories did control most of the government posts; the Assembly had proved its arrogance; and worst of all, the depression had intensified—markets had dried up, the flow of money had almost ceased, and confidence in the country was at an all-time low. Something had to be done. Perhaps a massive gathering of people marching on Toronto would be enough to coerce the British government and the Lieutenant-Governor into making changes.

Head was kept informed of Mackenzie's round of meetings and his frequent disloyal utterances, but he chose to ignore them. He found it hard to believe that anyone would trust the obnoxious agitator. In his *Narrative* (1839), the book Head wrote on his administration, he made plain his contempt for Mackenzie.

He is without exception the most notorious liar in all our country. He lies out of every pore in his skin. Whether he be sleeping or waking, on foot or on horseback, talking with his neighbours or writing for a newspaper, a multitudinous swarm of lies—visible, palpable, and tangible—are buzzing and settling around him like flies around a horse in August.

Surely the last election had proved that the people wanted to maintain the British connection, just as the results in the second riding of York proved that Mackenzie was politically discredited. Besides, persecution of Mackenzie would only increase his popularity; no good would be served by muzzling him.

During that summer and the early fall at least 117 meetings were held—Mackenzie claimed there were 200—and the corresponding secretary of the vigilance committee attended half of them. He was wearing himself out trying to maintain the editorial standard of his paper, making long and arduous trips by horseback and wagon, and stirring up large meetings to a revolutionary pitch. Most of the gatherings were peaceful because the Tories chose to stay away—they looked down their noses at those who lowered themselves by following the fiery demagogue. However, at Esquesing on August 12 and Churchville on August 15, Tory Orangemen gathered to hurl abuse at Mackenzie as he spoke from an open wagon. The *Patriot* feared he would be assassinated, "as sure as he attempts to call another seditious meeting". A bodyguard of young zealots took to riding with Mackenzie between meetings. On one journey they participated in a hand-to-hand fight with a Tory gang while crossing the Humber River. A victory in Mackenzie's favour was reported.

The whole countryside was alive to Mackenzie's incitements to a show of force—even to a bloodless coup—but "business as usual" prevailed in the city of Toronto. Head was rather amused when respectable citizens like James Fitz-Gibbon bored him with tales of impending anarchy. In September a moderate Reformer, Charles Fothergill, tried without success to stir the Lieutenant-Governor to action by telling him of the meetings around his home territory near Rice Lake. But the election had proved to Head that all was as it should be between colony and Mother Country. The settlers might be destitute, noisy, and demonstrative. But disloyal, never! When it became obvious to British authorities that the Lower Canadians would rebel, Head happily and confidently sent all his troops downriver to help Colborne. In his memoirs Head tried to justify this move as a calculated plan to trap Mackenzie into a fatal blunder, but the fact remains that he left several thousand arms and ammunition in the City Hall under the guard of only two constables. Here was an open invitation to rebellion.

On October 9 Jesse Lloyd, the emissary between Upper and Lower Canadian radicals, rode furiously into Toronto to tell Mackenzie of an uprising that was about to take place in the lower province. He wanted to know if Upper Canadian Reformers would join their brothers. At nightfall Doel's brewery was the scene of a clandestine gathering of eleven people—and of an impassioned speech by the irrepressible Scot who had called them together. They sat dumbfounded while he spoke:

I said that the troops had left ... that Fort Henry was open and empty and a steamer had only to sail down to the wharf and take possession; that I had sent two trusted persons to the garrison that day and that it was also "to let"; that the Lieutenant-Governor had just come in from his ride and was now at home, guarded by one sentinel; and that my judgment was that we should instantly send for Dutcher's foundrymen and Armstrong's axe-makers, all of whom could be depended on, and, with them, go promptly to the Government House, seize Sir Francis, carry him to the City Hall—a fortress in itself—seize the arms and ammunition there, and the artillery, etc. in the old garrison; rouse our innumerable friends in town and country; proclaim a provisional government; send off the steamer of that evening to secure Fort Henry; and either induce Sir Francis to give the country an Executive Council responsible to a new and fairly chosen Assembly to be forthwith elected, after packing off the usurpers in the "Bread and Butter" Parliament, or, if he refused to comply, go at once for Independence and take the proper steps to obtain it.

Logical arguments, frantic pleadings, and angry threats—nothing could rouse his friends. Mackenzie was calling for rebellion and this was too decisive a step to take on the spur of the moment. Dr T.D. Morrison was worried that there might be an informer in their midst. Others were afraid that hasty action now would doom political freedom in Canada for decades. Still others wanted a peaceful march of all Reformers on the capital, not open rebellion against constitutional authority. Only Little Mac was prepared to burn his bridges behind him. He had been forced out of the British political system. There was now only one course—a coup d'état—and there would never be a better time to act than that very night. But when the meeting broke up, Mackenzie lacked majority support for his violent plan.

The next day meetings were held with Morrison, John Rolph, and Jesse Lloyd. Mackenzie was finally able to persuade the two doctors that rebellion was inevitable and that, considering the preoccupation of the British with Lower Canada and the absence of any troops in the city, it could be accomplished without a single shot being fired. Mackenzie assured them that a large force of "patriots" could be gathered to secure the city and that a Provisional Government could then be proclaimed. Rolph—the most distinguished lawyer, doctor, and parliamentarian in the province—would then be appointed leader. By nightfall Mackenzie had gained permission from his fellow conspirators to ascertain how many people would support this action—but he was not to organize a rebellion!

The first week of November Mackenzie rode into the countryside. But he deviated from the agreed-upon plan. To attract supporters he not only named Rolph and Morrison as co-conspirators, but, with the agreement of Lount and Lloyd, he actually set a date—December 7—for the uprising. When he returned to Toronto in the third week of November he claimed to have a list of 4,000 to 5,000 volunteers, and to have recruited as their commander a well-respected and courageous young man of some military experience—Anthony Anderson of Lloydtown.

Rolph was faced with a fait accompli. But he hesitated to assume leadership of the rebellion. Before assenting to Mackenzie's plan, he made his position clear: he would take part, but not until an experienced military commander was found, the rebellion was won, and a Provisional Government was declared. Mackenzie assured him that Colonel Van Egmond, a wealthy farmer in the Huron district and a battle-scarred veteran of the Napoleonic Wars, could be recruited.

Towards the end of November Egerton Ryerson, who was intimately acquainted with the rural Methodists, called upon Attorney-General Hagerman and gave him a detailed account of rebel organizations in Vaughan, Albion, and Gwillimbury townships. "Nonsense!" retorted Hagerman. "There are not fifty men in the whole province who would dare descend on the city of Toronto."

On November 24 Mackenzie left again for the farming country. At the home of a radical sympathizer near Hogg's Hollow he used a small printing-press to run off a handbill proclaiming "Independence". "Brave Canadians!" began the inflammatory sheet. Are we "poor, spiritless, ignorant peasants who were born to toil for our betters?"

If we do not rise and put down Head and his lawless myrmidons, they will gather all the rogues and villains in the country together . . . and then deliver our farms, our families, and our country to their brutality. To that it has come. We must put them down or they will utterly destroy this country.

Most settlers were horrified when they read such things as "get ready your rifles"—an unfortunate man who carried a copy of the handbill into a country gathering was almost lynched. But there was a sufficient number who were intrigued by talk of rebellion. They found encouragement in reports from Lower Canada in late November that a force of rebels under Dr Wolfred Nelson had driven off several companies of British troops.

INDEPENDENCE!

There have been Nineteen Strikes for Independence from European Tyranny, on the Continent of America. They were all successful! The Tories, therefore, by helping us will help themselves.

The nations are fallen, and thou still art young,
Thy sun is but rising when others have set;
And tho' Slavery's cloud o'er thy morning hath hung,
The full tide of Freedom shall beam round thee yet.

BRAVE CANADIANS! God has put into the bold and honest hearts of our brethren in Lower Canada to revolt—not against "lawful" but against "unlawful authority." The law says we shall not be taxed without our consent by the voices of the men of our choice, but a wicked and tyrannical government has trampled upon that law—robbed the exchequer—divided the plunder—and declared that, regardless of justice they will continue to roll their splendid carriages, and riot in their palaces, at our expense—that we are poor spiritless ignorant peasants, who were born to toil for our betters. But the peasants are beginning to open their eyes and to feel their strength—too long have they been hoodwinked by Baal's priests—by hired and tampered with preachers, wolves in sheep's clothing, who take the wages of sin, and do the work of iniquity, "each one looking to his gain in his quarter."

CANADIANS! Do you love freedom? I know you do. Do you hate oppression? Who dare deny it? Do you wish perpetual peace, and a government founded upon the eternal heaven-born principle of the Lord Jesus Christ —a government bound to enforce the law to

flocks that they should be obedient to a government which defies the law, and is therefore unlawful, and ought to be put down, yet God has opened the eyes of the people to the wickedness of these reverend sinners, so that they hold them in derision, just as God's prophet Elijah did the priests of Baal of old and their sacrifices. Is there any one afraid to go to fight for freedom, let him remember, that

God sees with equal eye, as Lord of all,
A Hero perish, or a Sparrow fall.

That the power that protected ourselves and our forefathers in the deserts of Canada—that preserved from the Cholera those whom He would—that brought us safely to this continent through the dangers of the Atlantic waves—aye, and who has watched over us from infancy to manhood, will be in the midst of us in the day of our struggle for our liberties, and for Governors of our free choice, who would not dare to trample on the laws they had sworn to maintain. In the present struggle, we may be sure, that if we do not rise and put down Head, and his lawless myrmidons, they will gather all the rogues and villains in the Country together—arm them—and then deliver our farms, our families, and our country to their brutality—to that it has come, we must put them down, or they will utterly destroy this country. If we move now, as one

less, and the remainder will go to improve bad roads and to "make crooked paths straight;" law will be ten times more cheap and easy—the bickerings of priests will cease with the funds that keeps them up—and men of wealth and property from other lands will soon raise our farms to four times their present value. We have given Head and his employers a trial of 45 years—five years longer than the Israelites were detained in the wilderness. The promised land is now before us—up then and take it—but set not the torch to one house in Toronto, unless we are fired at from the houses, in which case self-preservation will teach us to put down those who would murder us when up in the defence of the laws. There are some rich men now, as there were in Christ's time, who would go with us in prosperity, but who will skulk in the rear, because of their large possessions—mark them! They are those who in after years will seek to corrupt our people, and change free institutions into an aristocracy of wealth, to grind the poor, and make laws to fetter their energies.

MARK MY WORDS CANADIANS!

The struggle is begun—it might end in freedom—but timidity, cowardice, or tampering on our part, will only delay its close. We cannot be reconciled to Britain—we have humbled ourselves to the Pharaoh of England people, and whose orbit shows us that it is by the same human means whereby you put to death thieves and murderers, and imprison and banish wicked individuals, that you must put down, in the strength of the Almighty, those governments which, like these bad individuals, trample on the law, and destroy its usefulness. You give a bounty for wolves' scalps. Why? because wolves harrass you. The bounty you must pay for freedom (blessed word) is to give the strength of your arms to put down tyranny at Toronto. One short hour will deliver our country from the oppressor; and freedom in religion, peace and tranquillity, equal laws and an improved country will be the prize. We contend, that in all laws made, or to be made, every person shall be bound alike—neither should any tenure, estate, charter, degree, birth or place, confer any exemption from the ordinary course of legal proceedings and responsibilities whereunto others are subjected.

CANADIANS! God has shown that he is with our brethren, for he has given them the encouragement of success. Captains, Colonels, Volunteers, Artillerymen, Privates, the base, the vile lirelings of our unlawful oppressors have already bit the dust in hundreds in Lower Canada; and altho' the Roman Catholic and Episcopal Bishops and Archdeacons, are bribed by large sums of money to instruct their

wishes—a government of equal laws—religion pure and undefiled—perpetual peace—education to all—millions of acres of lands for revenue—freedom from British tribute—free trade with all the world—but stop—I never could enumerate all the blessings attendant on independence!

CANADIANS! The struggle will be of short duration in Lower Canada, for the people are united as one man. Out of Montreal and Quebec, they are as 100 to 1—here we reformers are as 10 to 1—and if we rise with one consent to overthrow despotism, we will make quick work of it.

Mark all those who join our enemies—act as spies for them—fight for them—or aid them —these men's properties shall pay the expense of the struggle—they are traitors to Canadian Freedom, and as such we will deal with them.

CANADIANS! It is the design of the Friends of Liberty to give several hundred acres to every Volunteer—to root up the unlawful Canada Company, and give FREE DEEDS to all settlers who live on their lands—to give free gifts of the Clergy Reserve lots, to good citizens who have settled on them—and the like to settlers on Church of England Glebe Lots, so that the yeomanry may feel independent, and be able to improve the country, instead of sending the fruit of their labour to foreign lands. The 57 Rectories will be at once given to the people, and all public lands used for Education, Internal Improvements, and the public good. £100,000 drawn from us in payment of the salaries of bad men in office, will be reduced to one quarter, or much

Up then, brave Canadians! Get ready your rifles, and make short work of it; a connection with England would involve us in all her wars, undertaken for her own advantage, never for ours; with governors from England, we will have bribery at elections, corruption, villainy and perpetual discord in every township, but Independence would give us the means of enjoying many blessings. Our enemies in Toronto are in terror and dismay—they know their wickedness and dread our vengeance. Fourteen armed men were sent out at the dead hour of night, by the traitor Gurnett, to drag to a felon's cell, the sons of our worthy and noble minded brother departed, Joseph Sheppard, on a simple and frivolous charge of trespass, brought by a tory fool; and though it ended in smoke, it shewed too evidently Head's feelings. Is there to be an end of these things? Aye, and now's the day and the hour! Woe be to those who oppose us, for "In God is our trust."

Mackenzie's Independence handbill, printed in November 1837.

The Toronto Tories saw the Independence handbill and finally became concerned. On Saturday, December 2, a group met at Government House; among those present were Head, Hagerman, Judge Jones, the Honourable William Allan, Solicitor-General Draper, R.B. Sullivan, Chief Justice Robinson, and Colonel Allan Napier MacNab. They talked worriedly about the fear that was being created by rumours of rebellion. When FitzGibbon burst into the meeting exclaiming over reports of large-scale pike-making in the north, he was pooh-poohed—though to appease him they told him to organize two militia regiments and made him Acting Adjutant-General with orders to calm the city. Then, just in case there was some truth in FitzGibbon's tale, a warrant was issued for Mackenzie's arrest.

That same day, as MacNab boarded the night steamer for his home in Hamilton, Rolph heard him say that he planned to organize the Gore militia. Rolph, who didn't want any fighting, sent someone the next morning to David Gibson's house in Willowdale to suggest that, in view of developments in Toronto, it was imperative that the rebellion be moved up three days: from Thursday, December 7—the date set by Mackenzie and Lount—to Monday, December 4. By the time the oral message reached Gibson, and then Lount in Simcoe later that day, the suggestion had become an order. Lount immediately began to organize small groups and, with Anderson, head them south to the rendezvous point at Montgomery's tavern.* Neither Mackenzie nor Rolph knew anything of the change in plans.

Meanwhile Silas Fletcher, who had acted as a messenger

---

* A large inn on the west side of Yonge Street north of Toronto (at present-day Montgomery Avenue, north of Eglinton). On Friday, December 1, it had been leased to John Linfoot by John Montgomery.

between Rolph and Mackenzie, arranged a meeting for them on Monday at the home of James Price, several miles north of Toronto. When Rolph arrived at 1 p.m. he and David Gibson (who had come with Mackenzie) told Mackenzie they wanted to call the whole thing off. Lower Canadian rebels were being routed; if the troops returned to Toronto they would lose their chance to carry out plans for a quick and easy take-over of the city. Mackenzie was by now determined to proceed and nothing Rolph could say in their two-hour meeting would change his mind. Reluctantly Rolph agreed to await events and play his part later as planned.

It was not until late in the afternoon that Mackenzie heard that Anderson and Lount were on their way south with an armed force. He was beside himself. How could a potent force be organized on such short notice? Proper arrangements had not yet been made to have food, arms, and ammunition waiting for these men when they arrived at the tavern. Mackenzie's first reaction was to think of ways to stall the rebellion until Thursday, the day Van Egmond had said he would join Mackenzie at Montgomery's tavern.

Lount and Anderson spent Monday gathering men and marching over forty miles through early-December mud to the tavern. Mackenzie was waiting and wanted them to attack immediately. Lount would have no part of such rash action; as yet there were only 150 men and they needed rest. More were expected throughout the night and by morning there should be enough for an attack. Unfortunately John Linfoot, who now ran the tavern, would not co-operate with the rebels and supply food. Neither would Montgomery, who was still living in the tavern; he was annoyed because he had not been consulted about the rebellion.

Around 10 p.m. Mackenzie became so tense that he gave

John Montgomery

up his attempts to rest and rode south towards the city to investigate its defences. Anthony Anderson, Joseph Sheppard, and two others volunteered to go with him. Before leaving, Mackenzie placed three manned roadblocks across Yonge Street at different locations near the tavern to prevent loyalists from riding into Toronto to warn the inhabitants of the rebels' presence. Shortly two men were to die.

The first casualty was Colonel Moodie, veteran of the War of 1812 and a staunch loyalist. He and several friends had observed armed men riding towards Toronto; they decided to come south and warn Sir Francis of their suspicions. By the time Moodie arrived at the tavern roadblocks, all but two of his companions had thought better of the enterprise and returned home. On encountering the first two guards, Moodie and his friends burst their way through unharmed, but were then halted. When challenged by the sentries to stop, Moodie shouted from his horse: "Who are you? Who dares stop me on the Queen's highway?" Angrily he fired his pistol. The return fire knocked him off his horse and mortally wounded him. Farm boys who had been expecting to take Toronto without a shot were shocked to see Moodie lying before them, his life slowly ebbing away. They carried him to the tavern, tried to make him comfortable, and watched horrified and helpless for two hours as he suffered and died.

Meanwhile in the moonless pitch-black night Mackenzie and his little band made their way to Gallows Hill (at present-day Yonge and St Clair),* where they encountered Alderman John Powell of the noted Powell family and Archibald Macdonald, who had rather carelessly ridden out

---

* In earlier days there had been a high-banked gorge at this point of the wagon-road, across which a tree had fallen. The tree once lent itself to a suicide by hanging; thus the name.

A nineteenth-century impression of the beginning of [...]

ADRIAN = SHAR[...]

A nineteenth-century impression of the escape of John Powell.

of Toronto to reconnoiter. The two men were arrested by the rebels at gunpoint. When asked for their weapons, the prisoners declared that they had none and Mackenzie refused to search them. In his *Narrative* of the rebellion Mackenzie recorded his words. "As you are my townsmen and men of honour, I would be ashamed to question your words by ordering you to be searched." Considering that he was responsible for the success or failure of the rebellion and that these "men of honour" despised him, Mackenzie was being foolish indeed. Captain Anderson and Sheppard were sent back to Montgomery's tavern with the prisoners while Mackenzie continued down the hill.

No sooner did he reach the bottom than Mackenzie heard hoofbeats pounding down Yonge Street from behind. Mackenzie and his two men stopped to see who was approaching them in the dark. It was Powell and Macdonald. Mackenzie screamed at them to halt. When the two loyalists did not stop, he fired—and missed. Suddenly Powell reined in his horse, took aim at Mackenzie's face from close range, and squeezed the trigger. His shot misfired. Before the rebels could regain their composure, Powell and Macdonald quickly rode on. They split up and only Macdonald was recaptured— at the Bloor toll-gate.

Not long after, Powell was at the door of Government House demanding to see Sir Francis. When he was refused admission he forced his way in and strode upstairs to Head's bedroom. The puffing alderman's fat red face and heaving chest told his story. After glancing at Powell, the sleepy Lieutenant-Governor jumped out of bed.

On his way back to Montgomery's tavern Mackenzie came across the corpse of Anthony Anderson, who had been shot by Powell. The man who had been chosen to inspire and lead the rebels in an early attack on Toronto was dead. A dejected Mackenzie carried the news back to his men who were milling in and around the tavern.

That night at the tavern several hundred rebels had a supper of bad whisky while a ranting and raving Little Mac urged them to fight to the death on the morrow. With the capable Anderson dead, it seemed all too likely that this was what they would have to do. Suddenly they heard the sound of pealing bells coming from the city.

The alarm brought all of Toronto out of bed. Head wrote later:

I walked along King Street. . . . The stars were shining bright as diamonds in the black canopy over my head. The air was intensely cold and the snow-covered planks that formed the footpaths of the city creaked as I trod upon them. The principal bell of the town was in an agony of fear and her shrill irregular monotonous little voice, strangely breaking the serene silence of night, was exclaiming to the utmost of its strength—Murder! Murder! Murder! and much worse!

On his own initiative Judge Jones recruited thirty men and with them spent the rest of the night guarding the northern approaches to Toronto (south of present-day Bloor Street). Two to three hundred others, among them most of the town's prominent Tories, young and old, volunteered for action. Dispatch riders were hurriedly sent off to warn militia colonels in Gore, Midland, and Newcastle Districts.*

By Tuesday morning Head had worked himself into a frenzy worrying lest the arms and ammunition in the City Hall fall into rebel hands. FitzGibbon, when he suggested to the distraught Lieutenant-Governor that an immediate offen-

---

* From earliest times the province was divided into districts for judicial and military purposes.

sive be launched against Machenzie, was ordered to guard the hall and forget the rebels. Using sound military judgement, FitzGibbon instead sent Sheriff Jarvis and twenty-seven men out to replace Jones' picket. By noon the citizens had barricaded the town's main buildings—the government offices, the bank, and the land company office—all obvious targets of the rebels. Doors and windows were protected by two-inch planking looped in several places for muskets.

The town and provincial authorities were upset when, out of an adult male population of two to three thousand, only several hundred came forward to fight. Toronto was Tory, but voting was not the same as bearing arms. Many wanted to wait and see which side was going to win. Also, Toronto was a commercial town and Reformers, radicals, and rebels bought as many goods as the Tories.

Head realized his predicament and decided to stall until the militia from the rural communities arrived. At this point the city did not know the real strength of the rebels but rumours had so exaggerated their numbers and fire-power that there was little hope for a loyalist victory. Accordingly a truce mission was organized and Robert Baldwin and John Rolph—men highly respected by both Tories and Reformers— agreed to ride to the city limits and attempt a reconciliation with Mackenzie. Rolph, his true allegiance still not known to the government, had hesitated; but he committed himself to the team lest his complicity be suspected if he refused.

That morning Mackenzie began to crack under the strain of the impending battle. "Little Mac conducted himself like a crazy man all the time we were at Montgomery's," one of his volunteers said after the rebellion. "He went about storming and screaming like a lunatic, and many of us felt certain he was not in his right senses. He abused and insulted several of the men without any shadow of cause, and Lount had to go round and pacify them by telling them not to pay any attention to him, as he was hardly responsible for his actions."

Mackenzie lacked a commander for his forces. Colonel Van Egmond was not due to arrive until Thursday morning and Lount refused to take over. There was still no food for the hordes of hungry men at the tavern and Montgomery remained adamant in his refusal to find supplies. Mackenzie was livid. Lount and Gibson were finally able to enlist Montgomery's help and six groups of men set out to forage the district under his guidance.

The rebels held consultations throughout Tuesday morning, until Mackenzie, in a state of wild impatience, agreed to lead them in an attack. Around 11 a.m., with their "general" mounted on a small white horse and their numbers swollen to almost eight hundred, they slowly set out southward. The force was split up under Mackenzie and Lount; each would enter the city by a different route and meet at Osgoode Hall (at present-day Queen Street and University Avenue).

Near the brow of Gallows Hill Mackenzie became sidetracked at the home of James Howard, the Postmaster. He had gone to Toronto, and his wife, son, and daughter were startled to see coming towards their house a band of armed desperados

headed by a man on a small white horse, almost a pony, who turned out to be the commander-in-chief, Mackenzie himself. He wore a greatcoat buttoned up to the chin and presented the appearance of being stuffed. (In talking among themselves, the men intimated that he had on a great many coats as if to make himself bullet-proof.) To enable the man on the white pony to enter the lawn, his men wrenched off the *fence boards; he entered the house without knocking, took possession of the sitting-room where Mrs and Miss Howard and her brother were sitting, and ordered dinner to be got ready for fifty men. Utterly astonished at such a demand, Mrs Howard said she could do nothing of the kind. After abusing Mr Howard for some time—who had incurred his dislike by refusing him special privileges at the post office— Mackenzie said Howard had held his office long enough and that it was time somebody else had it. Mrs Howard at length referred him to the servant in the kitchen; which hint he took and went to see about dinner himself. There happened to be a large iron sugar-kettle in which was boiling a sheep killed by dogs shortly before. This they emptied and refilled with beef from a barrel in the cellar. A baking of bread just made was also confiscated and cut up by a tall thin man named Eckhart from Markham. While these preparations were going on, other men were busy in the tool-house mending their arms which consisted of all sorts of weapons, from chisels and gouges fixed on poles to hatchets, knives, and guns of all descriptions. About [one] o'clock there was a regular stampede and the family were left quite alone, much to their relief—with the exception of a young Highland Scotchman mounting guard. He must have been a recent arrival from the old country as he wore the blue jacket and trousers of the seafaring men of the Western Isles. Mrs Howard, seeing all the rest had left, went out to speak to him, saying she regretted to see so fine a young Scotchman turning rebel against his Queen. His answer was: "Country first, Queen next!"**

The reason for the abrupt departure of Mackenzie and his men from the Howard home was the arrival of a message

---

*This account is by Allan McLean Howard, quoted in Samuel Thompson, *Reminiscences of a Canadian Pioneer.*

saying that Lount had received a truce mission on Yonge Street. Rolph and Baldwin, and a few other men bearing a flag of truce, had approached Lount on Gallows Hill and conveyed Head's assurance that an amnesty would be granted if all the rebels dispersed immediately. The rebels held a conference, which Mackenzie joined when he arrived. They rejected the oral proposal and asked that it be put in writing. Mackenzie's *Narrative* says that he demanded "Independence" from the Lieutenant-Governor and requested an answer within an hour. While the rebels continued their march south to the toll-gate, Rolph and Baldwin rode on to report to Head.

In the meantime Head's confidence had been somewhat restored—probably because spies had informed him of the rebels' lack of arms and word had arrived that militia reinforcements were on their way. He would certainly not commit himself to writing or enter into any further communication with Mackenzie. The disillusioned truce team was forced to go north again to transmit Head's obstinate refusal to Lount and Mackenzie. The two rebels were waiting for them north of the toll-gate. When the message was delivered, Rolph was able to separate himself from Baldwin and communicate his own advice to Lount and Mackenzie. He told them that they should attack Toronto immediately. "Wend your way into the city as soon as possible, at my heels," he is reported to have said.* Mackenzie later claimed that Rolph told them to attack shortly after dark. In any case, when Rolph returned to the city he immediately met with his radical friends at Elliott's tavern and Doel's brewery and told

* Rolph's instruction was recorded in a statement made the next year by Timothy Parson, a Toronto merchant, who had by then left Canada. It is quoted in J.C. Dent, *The Story of the Upper Canadian Rebellion.*

them to support an attack by Mackenzie.

His excitement and mania steadily mounting since the previous evening, Little Mac was now almost frantic. A peaceful solution was no longer possible; a battle was inevitable. But the rebels were disheartened. "I seemed to feel that our enterprise was hopeless," one of them said later. No one was much inclined to march the few remaining miles into the city. The men again demanded food and many went off to find it.

At this point Mackenzie went on a rampage. The rebels had come to a house that Mackenzie believed was a rendezvous for loyalist spies. It belonged to Dr Horne, assistant cashier of the Bank of Upper Canada. Mackenzie dispatched Horne's large dog with a shovel, overturned the kitchen stove, and set fire to the house. He wanted to do the same to "Rosedale", Sheriff Jarvis's estate, but Lount was able to dissuade him.

Mackenzie then led his men back to the Howard farm where he demanded the meal he had ordered earlier.

Irritated at [Mrs Howard's] coolness, he got very angry, shook his horsewhip, pulled her from her chair to the window, bidding her look out and be thankful that her own house was not in the same state [as Horne's]. . . . Poor Lount, who was with them, told Mrs Howard not to mind Mackenzie but to give them all they wanted and they would not harm her.

The Howards provided boiled beef and whisky for the men, many of whom stayed until the next day.

On Tuesday afternoon a message was received from Rolph saying that an unprepared and almost undefended city awaited the rebels; he urged them to attack immediately. Arrangements were finalized for a march down Yonge Street.

A ragged little army of about 750 rebels—most of them wearing a badge of white cloth on their sleeve or lapel—set out from the Bloor toll-gate shortly after 6 p.m. Lount and his riflemen were in front. Behind, walking three abreast, followed two hundred pikemen with long iron-tipped staves and about fifty men armed with old muskets and shotguns. Trailing behind them was a larger group—several hundred farmers with pointed sticks and clubs. Mackenzie weaved crazily through the ranks, this way and that, on a dark bay horse.

Sheriff Jarvis and twenty-seven men had concealed themselves all day in William Sharpe's garden off Yonge Street (south-east of present-day Maitland Street). When the rebels appeared in the dark the crouching loyalists were ready for them. They waited until the rebels were within a hundred yards and then Jarvis gave the command. The loyalists opened fire—and promptly raced off into the dark. Lount's front men fired back, falling to the ground immediately afterwards to let the men behind fire next. But in the darkness and confusion the rear ranks thought their front line had been massacred. They fled in a panic. Mackenzie screamed at them to come back, but to no avail. More shots were fired by a few remaining rebels, but it soon became clear that they were firing at nothing: they had the field to themselves.

Later, at the toll-gate, Mackenzie was in a passion. Uttering threats and imprecations, he urged the men on to another attack. But nothing he said could persuade them to go back in the dark. They would wait for daylight.

A spirit of optimism and activity prevailed in Toronto. At 9 o'clock Tuesday night armed loyalists from the countryside had straggled into the city. A little later a steamer from

Hamilton brought Colonel MacNab and sixty volunteers from Gore District. By sunset on Wednesday a militia force of 1,500 men had been organized and drilled by Colonel FitzGibbon. Seeing that the scales were now tipped in favour of the government, Rolph and Morrison decided that the rebellion must be stopped. They sent a message to Mackenzie urging him to disband his force.

Mackenzie would do no such thing. He had gone too far now to abandon his plans for a descent on Toronto. Van Egmond was expected the next day, along with reinforcements. They might yet gain a victory!

Though new men were joining Mackenzie, his force was being depleted little by little because others were drifting off, discouraged by the little Scot's irresponsible excitability and the lack of food, weapons, and leadership. One of the men who didn't desert said: "We stayed with the others because we knew we should be arrested if we went home." His opinion of Mackenzie had altered. "We didn't stay out of any love for Mackenzie. We had found him out, and knew that he was useless for any purpose but *jaw*."

Mackenzie was so far from his normal upright self that he spent Wednesday playing the part of a bandit to raise money. He robbed the mail stage at gunpoint in front of the Peacock Inn on Dundas Street: the passengers were lined up, their money taken, and the mail bags pillaged. Mackenzie later scattered letters and newspapers from an upstairs window of the inn. After attacking and robbing other travellers and imprisoning them in the inn, he rode back to Montgomery's tavern.

In Toronto Dr Morrison was arrested at about 10 a.m. Wednesday morning as he returned from a call. Because of the doctor's close association with Mackenzie, Head felt he had sufficient evidence to press charges of treason. Rolph, when he heard about Morrison, decided there was no future for the rebellion. He picked up his medical bag, walked out of town (exchanging greetings with Chief Justice Robinson on the way), found a waiting horse at Dundas and Lot (Queen) Streets, and fled towards the American border.

In the meantime the militia were drilling in the market square. William Ryerson wrote his brother Egerton that he found

a large number of persons serving out arms to others as fast as they possibly could. Among others, we saw the Lieut.-Governor, in his everyday suit, with one double-barrelled gun in his hand, another leaning against his breast, and a brace of pistols in his leathern belt. Also Chief Justice Robinson, Judges Macaulay, Jones and McLean, the Attorney-General and Solicitor-General, with their muskets, cartridge boxes and bayonets, all standing in ranks as private soldiers under the command of Colonel FitzGibbon.

On Wednesday evening a meeting of government officials was held in Archdeacon Strachan's house. It was decided that an attack, led by MacNab, should be made on the rebels the next morning. Colonel FitzGibbon thought the command should have been given to him by right of his qualifications, to say nothing of the considerable time he had already spent preparing the city for an attack. He was in despair. Early the next morning, however, Head changed his mind and gave him the command. With volunteers pouring into town, and not enough officers to lead them, FitzGibbon now gave in briefly to despair of a different kind. Failure seemed inevitable. He sank to his knees and prayed. Then

I arose and hurried to the multitude, and finding one company formed, as I then thought providentially, I ordered

*it to be marched to the road in front of the Archdeacon's
house, where I had previously intended to arrange the force
to be employed. Having once begun, I sent company after
company and gun after gun, until the whole stood in order.*

Head gave the command to march at noon on Thursday.

Shortly after daybreak that morning the sixty-seven-year-
old Van Egmond, true to his word, arrived at Montgomery's
tavern, tired and hungry. Mackenzie, Lount, Gibson, Fletcher, Montgomery, and Van Egmond were soon engaged in a
heated argument. Mackenzie desired an all-out immediate
offensive. Van Egmond called this "stark madness". According to Gibson, at this point Mackenzie became so riled
that he threatened to shoot the colonel. Van Egmond was
resolute and maintained that they must bide their time in the
hope that more reinforcements would arrive. (As the rebels
argued, three steamers sailed into Toronto harbour bringing
more help for the loyalists.) After two hours of wrangling
Van Egmond won out. At about 10 a.m. Peter Matthews was
sent with eighty men to divert the government troops by
burning the Don River bridge to the east of the city. Van
Egmond hoped to prevent an attack on the tavern that day,
but he kept the main body of men with him in case the
stratagem did not work.

For the next two hours Montgomery's tavern was the
scene of confusion as the four hundred men waited and
wondered what would happen next. Van Egmond took the
time to review them and give some instructions in case of
attack. Once or twice there were rumours that "they" were
coming. Shortly after noon the piercing cry of bagpipes
was heard far away. In no time scouts were warning of a
massive troop movement up Gallows Hill. Silas Fletcher
shouted: "Seize your arms, men! The enemy's coming and no

mistake! No false alarm this time!" About 150 armed men were placed in a pine wood half a mile south of the tavern on the west side of Yonge. Another group was placed in the fields to the east. The rest, without arms, were left at the tavern.

Never before had little Toronto known such an exciting and dramatic event as the departure of the troops. The brightly shining sun, the clean and crisp December air, the rousing music of bagpipes and two bands, and the crowds of cheering citizens cast a happy glow on the warlike proceedings. Six hundred men led by MacNab, with Head and FitzGibbon close at hand, marched up Yonge Street. Behind came many women and children to witness the fray. Unknown to the rebels two other columns of loyalists were also converging on them—in groups of two hundred under Colonels W. Chisholm and S.P. Jarvis—along two sideroads east and west of Yonge Street.

The government troops came to a halt at the top of the hill (north of present-day Mount Pleasant Cemetery) and set up two cannon. "Presently our artillery opened their hoarse throats," wrote Samuel Thompson, "and the woods rang with strong reverberations. Splinters were dashed from trees —threatening, and I believe causing, more mischief than the shots themselves."

The skirmish lasted less than half an hour. There were few casualties. When the western flank under Colonel Chisholm suddenly appeared from the woods, the rebels beat a hasty retreat northward. The cannon were then moved north and aimed at the tavern. When they were fired, the tavern disgorged a flock of rebels who ran in all directions for their homes, over fences, through fields and woods, as fast as their legs could carry them.

The prisoners captured by the loyalists were given a stern lecture by the Lieutenant-Governor and then released and sent on their way. In a fit of revenge Head then ordered the tavern to be burned—an act that was grossly unfair to Linfoot the tenant, who was not implicated in the insurrection. Sir Francis, who took no other part in the skirmish, was highly pleased when the inn went up in flames.

As we sat on our horses the heat was intense; and while the conflagration was the subject of joy and triumph to the gallant spirits that immediately surrounded it, it was a lurid telegraph which intimated to many an anxious and aching heart at Toronto the joyful intelligence that the yeomen and farmers of Upper Canada had triumphed over their perfidious enemy, "responsible government".

Head later ordered the burning of David Gibson's house four miles to the north.

The rebel leaders headed for the safety of the United States. According to Mackenzie he had done his best to encourage his men to stay and fight and was one of the last to quit the tavern. Leaving behind a large carpetbag containing all his papers (including lists of names and addresses of most of the insurgents), he departed on horseback. At one point in his escape he was only thirty or forty yards ahead of his pursuers, yet he still managed to evade them. At first with a companion, then alone, he made his way west and south towards the American border.

6

Exile and Pardon

On Monday, December 11, 1837, Mackenzie left the adopted country to which he had given his every waking moment for the past thirteen years. In the early daylight hours a local sympathizer and Samuel Chandler, a guide, rowed him across the Niagara River to freedom. Mackenzie had made his way to the American frontier on horseback and on foot, going without food and sleep for long stretches of time, often pursued and on several occasions almost captured. In Trafalgar on Friday, December 8, he and a companion, Alan Wilcox, were almost caught by two bands of armed horsemen at Sixteen Mile Creek. They took to the bush, removed their clothes, and, holding them above their heads, waded naked through the icy creek swollen with early winter rains. "The cold in the stream," Mackenzie wrote later, "caused me the most cruel and intense sensation of pain I ever endured." He would never have reached safety without the help of people he encountered on his way. At some risk to themselves they fed, clothed, and sheltered him from bands of roving militia and vigilantes. (A reward of £1,000 had been posted for his capture.) Many were later imprisoned or persecuted for assisting him.*

---

*Samuel Chandler was banished to Van Dieman's Land but escaped and sailed around the world before returning home to his wife and eleven children.

PROCLAMATION.

BY His Excellency SIR FRANCIS BOND HEAD, Baronet, Lieutenant Governor of Upper Canada, &c. &c.

To the Queen's Faithful Subjects in Upper Canada.

In a time of profound peace, while every one was quietly following his occupations, feeling secure under the protection of our Laws, a band of Rebels, instigated by a few malignant and disloyal men, has had the wickedness and audacity to assemble with Arms, and to attack and Murder the Queen's Subjects on the Highway—to Burn and Destroy their Property—to Rob the Public Mails—and to threaten to Plunder the Banks—and to Fire the City of Toronto.

Brave and Loyal People of Upper Canada, we have been long suffering from the acts and endeavours of concealed Traitors, but this is the first time that Rebellion has dared to shew itself openly in the land, in the absence of invasion by any Foreign Enemy.

Let every man do his duty now, and it will be the last time that we or our children shall see our lives or properties endangered, or the Authority of our Gracious Queen insulted by such treacherous and ungrateful men. MILITIA-MEN OF UPPER CANADA, no Country has ever shewn a finer example of Loyalty and Spirit than YOU have given upon this sudden call of Duty. Young and old of all ranks, are flocking to the Standard of their Country. What has taken place will enable our Queen to know Her Friends from Her Enemies—a public enemy is never so dangerous as a concealed Traitor—and now my friends let us complete well what is begun—let us not return to our rest till Treason and Traitors are revealed to the light of day, and rendered harmless throughout the land.

Be vigilant, patient and active—leave punishment to the Laws—our first object is, to arrest and secure all those who have been guilty of Rebellion, Murder and Robbery.—And to aid us in this, a Reward is hereby offered of

One Thousand Pounds,

to any one who will apprehend, and deliver up to Justice, WILLIAM LYON MACKENZE; and FIVE HUNDRED POUNDS to any one who will apprehend, and deliver up to Justice, DAVID GIBSON—or SAMUEL LOUNT—or JESSE LLOYD—or SILAS FLETCHER—and the same reward and a free pardon will be given to any of their accomplices who will render this public service, except he or they shall have committed, in his own person, the crime of Murder or Arson.

And all, but the Leaders above-named, who have been seduced to join in this unnatural Rebellion, are hereby called to return to their duty to their Sovereign—to obey the Laws—and to live henceforward as good and faithful Subjects—and they will find the Government of their Queen as indulgent as it is just.

GOD SAVE THE QUEEN.

Thursday, 3 o'clock, P. M. 7th Dec.

☞ The Party of Rebels, under their Chief Leaders, is wholly dispersed, and flying before the Loyal Militia. The only thing that remains to be done, is to find them, and arrest them.

R. STANTON, Printer to the QUEEN'S Most Excellent Majesty.

Proclamation issued on Thursday, December 7, 1837, by Sir Francis Bond Head offering a reward of £1,000 for Mackenzie's capture.

Mackenzie escaped from the hands of the loyalists, but many of his associates were not so fortunate. Van Egmond, Lount, and Matthews were captured and suffered a tragic fate. The elderly Dutch colonel died in hospital after becoming ill in the cold, damp, filthy Toronto jail. On April 12, 1838, Lount and Matthews, despite numerous pleas of mercy and petitions bearing thousands of signatures, were hanged for treason on the common beside the King Street jail. Ninety-two of Mackenzie's supporters were transported to Van Dieman's Land (Tasmania), off the coast of Australia. Many others quit the province and moved to the United States.

On December 11, within hours of landing in New York State, Mackenzie was safe in Buffalo in the hands of friends. That evening, while Mackenzie rested, Doctor Chapin addressed a group of local citizens who had thronged to a public meeting in the theatre to hear the latest news from Canada. (A letter by Mackenzie, written at Montgomery's tavern on the eve of the insurrection, had been published in Buffalo that day.) Chapin excitedly told the overflowing audience of Canadian rebellion plans. He spoke of the popular uprisings that were expected throughout the province and of William Lyon Mackenzie and his daring escape to the United States. Chapin then announced dramatically that the fugitive was resting at his home at that very moment! Then he said: "He has thrown himself upon our protection. Will you protect him?" A thunderous applause from the crowd was their answer. "We never heard such a shout of exultation," reported the Buffalo *Commercial Advertiser*. Chapin urged everyone to come back next evening to hear Mackenzie himself speak. From among many volunteers, he chose six to protect the rebel from kidnappers.

Delighted to find himself the centre of so much attention, the next night Mackenzie deliberately played upon the emotions of his audience. He spoke for over an hour, describing in detail the causes of the rebellion, why it had failed thus far, his dramatic journey to freedom—all the while drawing parallels to *their* revolution against the British. He so enthralled his listeners that Thomas Jefferson Sutherland, a former military man and a self-styled adventurer, jumped up and declared that he would go to Upper Canada to help the patriots. Others followed suit. A pledge-sheet was circulated, a co-ordinating committee of thirteen set up, and the nearby Eagle Tavern designated as a meeting place for volunteers. The enthusiasm of the crowd convinced Mackenzie that the rebellion in Upper Canada might still be successful—with American help.

The news that Mackenzie was looking for American volunteers in Buffalo spread quickly. The word passed from town to town and from farm to farm that Canada was ripe for rebellion, that the Canadians were looking to the United States for help. Mackenzie received numerous letters from Americans throughout the northern states pledging their money, weapons, service, and advice. Among the volunteers who came to Mackenzie's side was Rensselaer Van Rensselaer, a West Point drop-out and the son of an influential New York general.

Mackenzie issued a Proclamation that stated at great length the "platform" of a Provisional Government, of which he was to be "chairman". The Proclamation, which offered a £500 reward for the capture of Sir Francis Bond Head, was issued in Buffalo on December 12, though it was dated "Navy Island, December 13, 1837". Navy Island was in British territory—in the fast-flowing Niagara River just above the

PROCLAMATION:

300 ACRES

Of the most valuable Lands in Cav
da, will be given to each VOLUNTEER who may join the Pat
orces now encamped on Navy Island, U. C.   Also,

$100 IN SILVER,

ayable on or before the 1st of Ma
ext.

By order of the Committee of th. Provincial Government.

W. L. MACKENZIE
Chairman Pro. Tem

Navy Island, Tuesday, Dec. 19th, 1837.

Mackenzie's second Navy Island Proclamation. The "Provincial Government" error was probably corrected by Mackenzie.

falls—and had an old naval dock where supplies could be landed. It was to be the home base for the "Friends of Liberty", who were preparing to strike against Upper Canada under the command of Van Rensselaer.

At Whitehaven, New York,* en route to Navy Island, Mackenzie and Van Rensselaer expected to meet two hundred and fifty volunteers for an attack on Canada. They were severely let down when they found only twenty-four. Mackenzie, downcast and disheartened, was said to have leaned against a cannon and shaken his head as if all was lost.

But circumstances brightened. Their small group occupied Navy Island on the night of December 14-15, and within two weeks they welcomed the arrival of nearly two hundred more men, most of them unemployed on account of the season and the economic depression and looking for adventure. A second Proclamation from Mackenzie promised each volunteer three hundred acres of fertile Canadian land and one hundred silver dollars on or before May 1. Food, medical supplies, blankets, guns, and money were sent by sympathizers who could not join them. Van Rensselaer happily directed the new arrivals, housed them in shacks, trained them, organized the defences, and distributed supplies—while constantly drinking brandy. In the meantime Mackenzie designed a tricolour—it had two stars to represent the independent states of Upper and Lower Canada—and a romantic "great" seal (twin stars again, with a new moon breaking through the surrounding darkness and the popular revolutionary words: Liberty—Equality).

The government of Upper Canada was now on a full-scale alert. Militia poured into Toronto and were immediately assigned to trouble spots throughout the province. A few

* On Grand Island in the Niagara River, ten miles from Buffalo.

hundred rebels led by Dr Charles Duncombe were easily dispersed by the militia in the London District; many of them fled to Detroit and Buffalo. The presence of refugees—especially Mackenzie—had been causing great excitement south of the border and Canadian authorities were becoming apprehensive. Colonel Allan MacNab was sent by the Lieutenant-Governor to Chippewa, immediately across the river from Navy Island, where he commanded a force of some 2,500 men. Commander Andrew Drew, R.N., a veteran of the Napoleonic Wars, was chosen to head a naval brigade. Sir Francis himself reviewed the militia at Chippewa. When MacNab asked for permission to attack Navy Island, Head refused to give it to him. He did not want to provoke a war with the United States by attacking the Americans on the island.

Nevertheless MacNab did strike at the Navy Island enterprise. For two days a small American steamer, the *Caroline,* had been ferrying weapons, men, and supplies to the island. (On one of her trips she had taken Isabel Mackenzie to join her husband.) Having received the weapons, the men on Navy Island proceeded to fire on the Canadian shore and continued to do so throughout the 29th. In the early-morning darkness of the 30th, Commander Drew, under orders from MacNab, cut the *Caroline* loose from her moorings at Fort Schlosser (the American landing opposite the island), set her afire, and towed her out to midstream. The empty boat caught upon a shoal, the fire died out, the copper bottom and engine sank, and the few charred remains drifted over the falls. While MacNab had succeeded in temporarily cutting off supplies to the island, the effect of the burning of the *Caroline* was that more Americans joined Mackenzie's side—to them it was an act of foreign aggression.

Mackenzie's small Navy Island army (300 to 400) was not a serious military threat to Upper Canada but it was a continuing source of tension between Britain and the United States.* The Americans, because of their neutrality laws, were embarrassed by Mackenzie's proximity and the involvement of their citizens in his plans. One suspects that the American government quietly exercised its restraining muscle when another ferry boat, bid on at an auction by the "Friends of Liberty", was sold instead to General Scott of New York State.

Finally a new boat was found and preparations for war continued on Navy Island. But the wintry weather soon diminished everyone's enthusiasm. The wooden shacks in which the men lived were cold and damp; the action for which they had volunteered was slow in coming. Isabel, the only woman on the island, and a source of courage and cheer to everyone, was forced to leave for home because of ill health. Mackenzie accompanied her as far as Buffalo. There he was arrested for a breach of American neutrality laws but was released on $5,000 bail and allowed to return to the island.

Mackenzie felt that he was becoming less and less significant, that Americans were taking over his revolution. He bickered with Van Rensselaer constantly. Navy Island was being subjected to heavy fire from the Canadian shore. Van Rensselaer, whose dreams of fame and glory had found no satisfaction, decided that the time had come to quit the project. On January 14, under a heavy barrage from the Canadian forces on shore, he left with his men, only to be

---

* The American press stirred up public opinion, Britain was denounced at meetings, and some congressmen and New York politicians made warlike statements. President Van Buren, seeking to maintain peace with Britain, took no action.

arrested when he touched American soil. Mackenzie evac-
uated at the same time and headed for Rochester. Navy
Island fell into the hands of the Canadian militia.

Many of the volunteers continued the fight under the
direction of various American Patriot groups.* In 1838 they
organized raids on Upper Canada. The most notable of these
occurred at Bois Blanc (Amherstburg) in January under
"Generals" Henry S. Handy and Thomas Jefferson Sutherland; at Fighting Island in the Detroit River on February 25
under Donald McLeod, a former Brockville schoolmaster; at
Pointe au Pelé in late February under Sutherland and Colonel
Bradley, an Ohio sympathizer; and at Prescott in mid-Novem-
ber under Nils Von Schoultz, a brave thirty-one-year-old
Polish adventurer. The Battle of Windmill Point at Prescott
was by far the most serious of these incidents—at least one
hundred were killed. After this attack President Van Buren
cracked down on American raiders, though in December
there was one more major raid—on Windsor—in which
twenty-five rebels were killed and much Canadian property
was destroyed.

Mackenzie did his best to fan hostilities. He lived entirely
for the invasion effort, travelling about and holding inflammatory meetings whenever possible. From January to March
he spoke in Plattsburg, Philadelphia, New York, and Lockport
(where he helped found the Canadian Refugee Relief Association to locate all expatriates and aid them if necessary). He
established a residence in New York City where his family
joined him in May 1838. There, that same month, he started
another newspaper, Mackenzie's Gazette—a "gospel of liberty

---

* Such as the "Patriot Army of the North West". Various lodges or secret societies
were also formed by exiled Canadians and Americans living in states bordering the
Great Lakes.

to sympathizers on both sides of the border"—which had far more readers than paid subscribers. The paper was devoted almost entirely to news of Canada and the British Empire. Nearly every edition carried stories—"The Burning of the *Caroline*", "History of Insurrection in the Canadas"—to encourage popular feeling against the British colonies to the north.

On September 5, 1838 Mackenzie declared his intention of becoming an American citizen. Throughout the fall of 1838 he kept up his public-speaking tour of major American cities, but in February 1839 he moved to Rochester, probably to be closer to action at the border. He immediately proceeded to stir up trouble. He called a convention to promote Canada's independence and set up—with his fellow exile, John Montgomery, who was keeping another inn—an association of Canadian refugees.

Three months later, Mackenzie was brought to trial.* He was charged with "setting on foot a military enterprise at Buffalo, to be carried on against Upper Canada, a part of the Queen's dominions, at a time when the United States were at peace with Her Majesty; with having provided the means for the prosecution of the expedition; and with having done all this within the dominion and territory, and against the peace, of the United States."

The trial was held in Canandaigua, New York; it began on June 19, 1839 and lasted two days. Mackenzie defended himself in his old colourful and dramatic way. He spoke of "that girl", Queen Victoria, and the unlawful British yoke that it was Canada's fate to bear; he said that he and his friends were "poor exiled refugees", and told of their

* The Americans appeared reluctant to try him; his case had been postponed several times since June 1838.

admiration for the free institutions of the United States—especially the judiciary; and he gave overwhelming approval to what he thought was the obvious American desire to envelop Upper Canada. "Why should there be deception used?" he asked. "You want Canada, I know it. I never yet talked seriously to an American who did not admit a desire to see European government removed from the North." For six hours he "enchanted the audience", and when he finished, commented the Rochester *Daily Democrat*, "if a vote had been taken for his conviction or liberation he would have had a strong vote in his favour."

Mackenzie's appeal, however eloquent, did not sway the jury. After a two-and-a-half-hour deliberation they found him guilty. He was fined ten dollars and sentenced to eighteen months in prison, effective immediately. The judge passed what he considered a light sentence because, wrote the sympathetic Charles Lindsey, "the defendant had acted with a zeal which actuates men who, however mistaken, think they are right."

Mackenzie's hypertense and weary condition grew worse in Rochester jail. He was confined without exercise to a miserable third-floor cell—reached by a ladder through a trap door in the second-floor ceiling—close to a room provided for the city's street-walkers, whose comings and goings disturbed him. He became suspicious of everyone, especially his haggard, hook-nosed, sunken-eyed, filthy jailer, who he thought was trying to poison him. His older girls and Isabel visited Mackenzie regularly and brought him food and tea. He and his family received jeers and catcalls from the inmates, and indifferent treatment from the jailer; the girls sometimes had to pound on the downstairs door for as long as an hour before they were let out. No visitors were allowed into the jail after three in the afternoon or at any time on Sunday.

In December ninety-year-old Elizabeth Mackenzie took seriously ill. Her son was denied permission to go to her, but through the kind machinations of John Montgomery he was able to see her before she died. Montgomery was involved in a trial and had arranged for it to be conducted in Mackenzie's home; he then received permission to have Mackenzie appear as a witness. The magistrate delayed proceedings by arriving late so that Mackenzie could spend a few hours with his dying mother. Lindsey records that, as he was about to leave her bedside, the frail old woman raised herself to give him her blessing, then sank back and spoke no more. Three days before Christmas, Mackenzie watched her funeral procession pass his jail window. He was overcome with grief. They had lived under the same roof for most of Mackenzie's forty-four years. He was always proud of his courageous mother and never forgot that before her last illness she had walked to the jail four times to visit him.

Mackenzie's wife and seven children began to suffer more deprivations, although occasionally friends did send money to help them. To support his family during these miserable, frustrating months Mackenzie compiled and had published the *Caroline Almanack*, a highly mendacious booklet that was designed to please sensation-loving rebel sympathizers. The cover bore a picture of a flaming *Caroline* tilting over the falls; inside was Mackenzie's fabricated account of the fate of the empty vessel, which he said passed "with fearful speed towards the great falls in a blaze of flame, the elements of fire and water combining in their fury to send to eternity those who had hid themselves in the boat from the dagger of the assassin." He continued: "We witnessed the dreadful scene from Navy Island." In one of the malicious articles

Mackenzie wrote about his former colleagues, he exonerated himself and blamed Rolph, Morrison, and Lount for the failure of the rebellion. Elsewhere he wrote of tyranny and oppression in Upper Canada and said the Queen of England was "as keen for spilling . . . blood as her mad old grandfather Geo. 3rd."

Mackenzie continued to suffer in jail. He grew more and more depressed; unable to eat, he took sick. Dr John Smyles of Rochester certified that, because of Mackenzie's "highly susceptible nervous system", the jail was endangering his health. As a result, in April he was allowed daily walks outside. Meanwhile friends and sympathizers—for he still had many—were sending petitions on his behalf to the governor of New York and to President Van Buren.* In one of Mackenzie's own petitions to the President he promised to give up publishing his *Gazette*, which had been appearing occasionally in his absence, for the remainder of his term if he was pardoned and released. All these efforts succeeded in helping his cause. On May 10, 1840, after almost eleven months' confinement, Mackenzie was freed.

He returned to publishing his *Gazette*. Perversely he tried to establish rapport with Americans by attacking the political establishment—of the United States this time. But people were not interested and the paper did not sell well enough to afford him a living. In his disillusionment over its failure he began to have doubts about the American system of government, which he had once hailed as so grand and fair. In the last issue of the *Gazette*, published on December 23, 1840, he declared that power was passing into the hands of "an aristocracy, not of noble ancestry and ancient lineage, but of monied monopolists, land-jobbers, and heartless politicians".

* Lindsey states that there were 300,000 petitioners.

The types and presses were sold to provide money for his family, which increased a few weeks later with the arrival of a son named George.

Mackenzie tried hard to earn enough money to support his family—who often went for twenty-four hours without food. He attempted to set himself up as a lawyer but attracted no clients; then he failed to land an inspectorship on the Erie Canal. He tried unsuccessfully to obtain compensation from the United States government for expenses incurred by his trial and imprisonment. However when the Canadian Society in Cincinnati presented him with an offer to begin a democratic paper, he turned it down on the grounds that "if I have a heart it is in Canada with those who suffered for their principles, and there only will I be at home."

Mackenzie was still obsessed with his dream of an independent Canada and was prepared to sacrifice his last material possessions and the comfort of his family if it could be brought to fulfilment. On February 10, 1841, Britain enacted a union of Upper and Lower Canada to form the Province of Canada. In Mackenzie's view the one Canadian legislature was simply a more efficient means for Britain and the colonial Tories to dominate Canadian farmers, political reformers, and French Canadians. On April 17, 1841, Mackenzie began another newspaper, the *Volunteer,* which was supported by donations. (On its masthead was the two-starred rebel flag floating over Navy Island.) If he could not convince Canadians that a hoax had been perpetrated on them, then perhaps he might be able to promote a war between the United States and Canada.

In a vain attempt to do this, Mackenzie's *Volunteer* devoted much space to the case of Alexander McLeod, Deputy Sheriff of the Niagara District, who had been arrested while visiting the States and charged with the murder of Amos Durfee, an American who had been shot during the capture of the *Caroline.* The British were indignant that an individual militiaman should be held criminally responsible for carrying out military orders given to him in time of war. There was much soul-searching in Britain and the United States over the justice of the charge. Mackenzie fought to have McLeod convicted and even covered the trial himself. McLeod, however, was ably defended by the famous Daniel Webster and acquitted.

Mackenzie's friend, Dr John Smyles—now a reporter for the New York *Herald* in Canada—agreed to cover the meetings of the Canadian legislature for Mackenzie's paper. When he passed around copies of the *Volunteer,* which was not allowed to travel through the mails, members rejected them. No one appeared to be too interested in Mackenzie's aims in publishing his paper. The *Volunteer* folded on May 10, 1842, after nineteen issues.

Mackenzie's financial problems continued unabated. In the summer of 1841 he was forced to give the family's silver spoons to his landlord in lieu of rent; he also had his precious gold medal, the gift of his York constituents, melted down. (Of the $147 he received for the metal, a creditor claimed all but $16.) Somehow the family eked out an existence through the winter of 1841-2. Their Clinton Street home was cold and bare and they often went without food. Once they had a fire and lost some of their few pieces of furniture. Mackenzie wrote to his son James, now a printer in Lockport: "The more I see of this country, the more do I regret the attempt at revolution at Toronto."

Finally, worn down by hunger and pleurisy and by an overriding fear that someone would kidnap him and smuggle him into Canada to claim the £1,000 reward that still rested on his head, he admitted defeat. He had been "starved out" of Rochester. In June 1842, with two and a half dollars in his pocket, he moved his family to New York by way of the Erie Canal. He borrowed money to pay the moving expenses and $39 barge fare.

In the seven years Mackenzie spent in New York he shifted from job to job in search of a better income. He first worked as an actuary with the New York Mechanics' Institute. In his spare hours, to supplement his income, he began a book about the Irish community in New York, but he wrote no more than sixty pages. There were times when he did not have one cent to his name—though he somehow found the money to send his children to good schools. On September 8, 1842, he wrote: "My daughter Janet's birthday; aged thirteen.* When I came home in the evening, we had no bread—took a cup of tea without it." By the end of 1843 he had quit the Institute. Falling back on the only trade he enjoyed, he started another paper, the *Examiner,* which lasted only three issues.

Early in 1844 Mackenzie was introduced to the son of President Tyler, who arranged for him to be nominated for an Inspectorship of Customs at New York. Mackenzie was crestfallen when he learned that he was ineligible because he was "a British outlaw" and had attacked President Van Buren. But Tyler hinted that another equally lucrative position was available. Mackenzie then foolishly moved his family into a more pretentious house with a rent of $450 a year, saw to it that the children were well dressed, and hired an Irish servant girl to help Isabel. This standard of living was very difficult to maintain and for the winter the family was

* In 1852 Janet married Charles Lindsey, Mackenzie's future biographer.

forced to live in one room of the house because that was all they could afford to heat. After sitting up late to enjoy the evening fire, they would bundle themselves into two large double beds and stay there until well after sunrise. The good job never materialized. When Mackenzie was offered a $700-a-year clerk's job at the customs office, he took it. In July, weary but somewhat wiser, he moved his family into a less costly house.

Adversity and advancing age brought Mackenzie closer to his family than he had ever been before. He kept "reminiscences" of their problems on scraps of paper. In the winter of 1844 they were plagued with childhood diseases. Barbara and Helen came down with scarlet fever while George had whooping cough. A turkey dinner for Christmas brightened everyone's spirits. Little Isabel—the second child to be given her mother's name and the last-born of their thirteen children—was doing well.*

While working at the customs office Mackenzie read some papers and letters written by a former Collector of Customs Mr Jesse Hoyt, which revealed to Mackenzie's quick actuarial eye that Hoyt had embezzled $250,000. Mackenzie could not ignore evidence of such corruption. He resigned his job on June 1, 1845, borrowed some money to meet his current expenses, and retired to write an exposé of Hoyt and his accomplice. The result was *The Lives and Opinions of Benjamin Franklin Butler, United States District Attorney for the Southern District of New York, and Jesse Hoyt, Counsellor at Law, formerly Collector of Customs for the Port of New York*. Wishing to avoid a court action, Mackenzie assigned the copyright to his publishers, thereby missing

---

* In 1872 Isabel married John King, a prominent lawyer and author. They became the parents of a future prime minister of Canada, William Lyon Mackenzie King.

out on the large royalties: the book sold over 50,000 copies.

Finding himself more deeply in debt than ever, and taking advantage of the publicity from his book on Hoyt, he wrote *The Life and Times of Martin Van Buren,* which severely attacked the former president. He sold the copyright for $1,000 late in 1845.

In 1846 Mackenzie was asked by Horace Greeley, the editor of the New York *Tribune,* to write a series of articles on meetings in Albany to revise the State constitution. These lasted through to October and Mackenzie stayed on until April 1847 to report on the proceedings of the State legislature. He was not impressed when he saw in action the type of democracy he had been advocating for the last twenty years. "After what I have seen here," he wrote to his son James, "I frankly confess to you that, had I passed nine years in the United States before instead of after the outbreak, I am very sure I would have been the last man in America to be engaged in it."

In 1848 Mackenzie was fired by the *Tribune* when one of Greeley's partners took offense at the tone of Mackenzie's political articles; but he was rehired. Family tragedies continued to sadden his life. His eldest daughter, Barbara, had had to be committed to the Bloomingdale Asylum for the Insane. He wrote on May 4: "Visited Barbara . . . on the occasion of her birthday—she be then 21; sat and walked through the grounds with her." Nine days later he took his wife and two sons to visit but found her "troubled and bitter". "Poor Barbara!" he lamented. He became even more depressed in July when his twelve-year-old daughter Margaret—affectionately known as Totty—died after a long illness. He never adjusted to her death and always wore her gold watch around his neck.

William Lyon Mackenzie in middle age

For the past few years Mackenzie had entertained some hope of returning to Canada, where he had been prosperous and popular. At the age of fifty-three there was little chance that he would do well in the United States. Rolph, Montgomery, Gibson, Duncombe, and Papineau had all been given permission to return to Canada and Mackenzie requested the same privilege. He wrote to the Colonial Office:

Had the violent movements in which I and many others were engaged on both sides of the Niagara proved successful, that success would have deeply injured the people of Canada, whom I then believed I was serving at great risks; .... I have been sensible of the errors committed during that period to which the intended amnesty applies. No punishment that power could inflict or nature sustain would have equalled the regrets I have felt on account of much that I did, said, wrote, and published; but the past cannot be recalled.

Mackenzie's pardon was finally granted under a general amnesty passed in February 1849 by the Reform ministry of Robert Baldwin. To test public opinion in Canada, before bringing his family back, he visited Montreal and Toronto alone.

He could not have picked a worse time. The legislature, meeting in Montreal, had just passed the Rebellion Losses Bill by which compensation would be paid to anyone, including rebels, for losses incurred during the rebellion. The Tories were furious. They mobbed the Governor-General, rioted in the streets of Montreal, and burned the parliament buildings to the ground. When Mackenzie visited the legislative library, Colonel Prince, a volatile Tory from Windsor, recognized him and threatened to kick him downstairs if he did not leave immediately. He did.

Toronto was organized in its opposition to Little Mac's

return. The *Examiner* put out an "extra" on March 23 in which it recounted the violence that Mackenzie's visit had precipitated the night before. "About 9 o'clock p.m. an assemblage of unshaven, dirty-looking, half-intoxicated men and ragged boys" gathered on Yonge Street. Shortly a crowd of 1,500—attracted by a false fire alarm—were burning barrels of tar in front of John Macintosh's house where Mackenzie was staying. An effigy of Mackenzie was set on fire and to the cries of "Colonel Moodie!", bricks, stones, and sticks were thrown at the house, breaking many panes of glass. Another Toronto paper reported (recalling to mind how Little Willie tormented his schoolmaster) that when the effigy was paraded outside Macintosh's, "some person inside, with the most extraordinary folly, danced a doll at the window in evident ridicule and contempt of those outside." Mackenzie had never been cowed by a show of force against him and was not intimidated now.

In Mackenzie's twelve-year absence the city of Toronto had continued its rapid growth. The population—swelled largely by Irish and Scottish immigrants—was now almost 25,000, more than double its pre-rebellion days. Gas lights had been installed on the main thoroughfares and two miles of boardwalks lined King Street, which was now macadamized. In 1846 Mayor William Henry Boulton had sent the first commercial telegram from the City Hall on Front Street. A one-man mail delivery service was instituted for those who were willing to pay (others still had to walk to the post office). Toronto had lost the seat of provincial government in the Act of Union, which brought about a two-capital system: Quebec (after the Montreal riot) and Kingston alternated on a yearly basis. Nevertheless the city newspapers still found many political issues to complain about and quarrel over.

Toronto was now served by two Reform newspapers: James Lesslie's *Examiner* and George Brown's *Globe*.

In May 1850 Mackenzie moved his family back to Toronto. The inhabitants quietly ignored him. The rebellion was past history—a shame to be forgotten. The County of York, however, was still grateful to Mackenzie for his past services and came forward with a gift of £300. He was also fortunate to receive money owing him from 1835 when he was a director of the Welland Canal—an ironic boon, considering that in 1838 he had assisted in delivering explosives to blow up some installations on the canal.

Mackenzie's main interest continued to be politics; he still hated to be on the sidelines. In the spring of 1851 there was a by-election to fill a vacant seat in Haldimand County. Mackenzie put up his name and won (over George Brown of the *Globe*). Now in a position to face old foes, he brought forward a motion in the Assembly to abolish the Court of Chancery—a project that Robert Baldwin had reorganized two years before—and experienced a moment of glory when it was passed. The Reform ministry broke up and Baldwin retired from public life.

Mackenzie then turned against Rolph, who had joined the Assembly with Mackenzie's blessing soon after Baldwin left. Mackenzie became bitter when Rolph refused to support his claim for $12,000 under the Rebellion Losses Bill, and repeatedly tried to persuade the Assembly and the press that Rolph was a traitor because of his role in the flag-of-truce mission during the rebellion. He had accused Rolph in the *Caroline Almanack* of treachery and criminal indiscretion during the rebellion; now he attacked him in yet one more newspaper—his last—called *Mackenzie's Weekly Message*, which first appeared in February 1853. David Gibson wrote to Rolph that Mackenzie "has been making brags that he is the only man that can break you down, and I have no doubt he will do all he can." But people did not take Mackenzie very seriously any more. The members of the Assembly merely tolerated him "out of consideration of his age and afflictions".

By now friends and foes alike were beginning to doubt Mackenzie's sanity. A contemporary historian, John Mac-Mullen, wrote that the *Weekly Message* was distinguished for "snappish and ill-natured articles, querulous complainings, and for being the receptacle of fantastic odds and ends, the fungi of an energetic and acute yet diseased and ill-balanced intellect." Mackenzie had always been erratic and volatile, but now these characteristics became more pronounced. His old friend James Lesslie was in charge of a subscription campaign to raise funds for the Mackenzie family. When Mackenzie learned that a considerable sum of money had been collected, he went to Lesslie to ask for enough cash for a trip to Scotland and Europe. Lesslie told him that he had no power to release any portion of the fund for this purpose. Mackenzie, in a fury, abused Lesslie. He ran paid advertisements declining any more subscriptions. However, with part of the money that had been raised, the committee was able to buy in 1859 a house for the Mackenzies on Bond Street.* There was enough left for a small monthly allowance.

In August 1858 Mackenzie retired his Haldimand seat in disgust over the fact that his constituents gave their support to a railroad line that he did not want. The last issue of the *Message* appeared in the fall of 1860. Thereafter Mackenzie's health steadily declined.

* This is Mackenzie House, owned by the City of Toronto and run by the Toronto Historical Board. It is open to the public.

The Mackenzie house on Bond Street, Toronto, as it looks today. It was originally part of a row of three houses.

In 1861 Mackenzie was $3,000 in debt and confined to his
Bond Street home. Charles Lindsey described him at the end
of his life:

*Whether he was himself aware of the extent to which his
health had failed, that the iron frame was so far shaken and
debilitated as it was, it is impossible to say. His tenacity of
life would probably prevent him from admitting to himself
the true state of the case; and though he often spoke of the
decline of his strength, he generally did so by way of inquiry
and with a view of eliciting the opinion of others on the
subject. It was a point on which he was morbidly sensitive;
and the last time he was out, before being confined to his
death-bed, he enquired anxiously of one of his daughters
whether people remarked that he was failing. When he did so,
he drew himself up in a more erect posture and walked with a
show of unwonted firmness, as if desirous to disprove an
impression that he dreaded.*

He grew weaker and weaker. Yet during his last illness he
stubbornly refused to obey the doctor's orders to take a
prescribed medicine. The quick temper faded, his mind
wandered, his eyes dulled. Tides of unconsciousness came
and went. He died on August 28, 1861.

At the Presbyterian service held four days later in Mackenzie's Bond Street house, the mourners included the mayor of
Toronto, numerous M.P.P.s, and seventy-eight-year-old John
Montgomery. A procession half-a-mile long followed the
body to the Toronto Necropolis, where William Lyon Mackenzie was buried in the north-east corner.

Sources and
Further Reading

Paperback editions are marked with an asterisk(*).

The first biographer of William Lyon Mackenzie was Charles Lindsey, his son-in-law. *The Life and Times of Wm. Lyon Mackenzie* (Toronto, 1863; paperback reprint, 2 vols, Toronto, 1971) is not only the primary source for Mackenzie's life but an extensive and conscientious presentation of details and documents. Lindsey, however, was not a detached biographer. Overly sympathetic to his subject and at times apologetic, he contributed to the public acceptance of Mackenzie as a misunderstood reformer, a sad figure of "shipwrecked hopes and overwhelming disappointment" who began an insurrection without which "there is no reason to suppose that the Province would yet have reached its present stage of advancement". Lindsey contributed to this erroneous theory and to other misconceptions. He presented Mackenzie as a dedicated supporter and advocate of responsible government, which he was not; he labelled all opponents of Mackenzie as Tories and thought of all Tories as members of the Family Compact; he failed to analyse the Tories and their point of view; and he accepted uncritically Mackenzie's own account of the rebellion. Though the book has many scholarly weaknesses and inaccuracies, it is nevertheless an interesting work from a period close to Mackenzie's own and contains useful information.

John Charles Dent, in *The Story of the Upper Canadian Rebellion* (2 vols, Toronto, 1885), applied himself to discrediting Mackenzie (and Lindsey's study) and produced a documented and scathing denunciation of his character and leadership ability. The Tories did not escape condemnation and were criticized for their intransigence and for scheming against democracy. The main value of Dent's book lies in its chronological account of the rebellion based on eyewitness reports and written records.

In the early 1900s the Lindsey family were able to obtain a court order preventing the publication of what they considered to be an unsympathetic biography by W.D. LeSueur—a testimony to the intensity of feeling about Mackenzie that still existed forty years after his death. A single copy of the book exists and is in the University of Toronto Library. LeSueur's study is scholarly and thorough, but he went to unnecessary extremes to find inconsistencies and contradictions in Mackenzie's ideas, arguments, and behaviour.

William Kilbourn's modern biography—*The Firebrand* (Toronto, 1959)—is an interesting and lively account not only of Mackenzie's career but of the atmosphere of his times. His study is impressionistic and concentrates more on Mackenzie's character than on the economic and political background. His amusing characterization of the Tories is extreme, but the overall portrait of Mackenzie is convincing and memorable.

Upper Canada was a backwater of civilization in the early nineteenth century and the pioneer newspapers filled a void created by the absence of schools, books, neighbours, literary societies, and social organizations. Editors of the period were allowed much licence, so their newspapers—and in particular those of William Lyon Mackenzie—are rewarding for the researcher. Mackenzie's papers reveal his political and economic ideas at various stages of his life. They were the *Colonial Advocate* (York, 1824-34), which provided much of the quoted material in this book; the *Constitution* (Toronto, July 4, 1836 to December 6, 1837); *Mackenzie's Gazette* (New York and Rochester, 1838-40); the *Volunteer* (Rochester, 1841-2); and *Mackenzie's Weekly Message* (Toronto, 1852-60). The rival publications are also necessary reading for a balanced view of Upper Canadian government and society: the *Upper Canada Gazette* (York/Toronto, 1743-1849?), the official government paper published by the King's Printer; the independent *Canadian Freeman* (1825-34) edited by Francis Collins; the Tory *Courier of Upper Canada* (1829-37) edited by George Gurnett; and the Tory *Patriot and Farmer's Monitor* (Kingston, 1828 and Toronto, after December 7, 1832) edited by Thomas Dalton; the independent *Canadian Correspondent* (York/Toronto, 1832-1837), edited by William John O'Grady, which amalgamated with the *Colonial Advocate* on November 4, 1834, to become the *Correspondent and Advocate;* and the *Christian Guardian* (York/Toronto, 1829-1925), a generally conservative paper, which was edited by Egerton Ryerson from 1829 to 1832, 1833 to 1835, and 1838 to 1840.

Among the books Mackenzie wrote are *Sketches of Canada and the United States* (London, 1833); *A New Almanack for the Canadian True Blues; with which is incorporated The Constitutional Reformer's Text Book; For the millenial and prophetical year of the Grand General Election for Upper Canada, and total and everlasting downfall of Toryism in the British Empire, 1834. By Patrick Swift, Esq., M.P.P. Professor of Astrology, York* (Toronto, 1834); *The Seventh Report from the Select Committee of the House of Assembly of Upper Canada on Grievances* (Toronto, 1835); *The Lives and Opinions of Benjamin Franklin Butler, United States District Attorney, and Jesse Hoyt, Counsellor at Law, formerly Collector of Customs for the Port of New York* (Boston, 1845); and *The Life and Times of Martin Van Buren* (Boston, 1846). *Mackenzie's Own Narrative of the Late Rebellion* (Toronto, 1838), written in the United States, is often erroneous and misleading. It was published in Canada by Charles Fothergill, who added his own editorial notes criticizing Mackenzie's record of the events and severely chastising the Tories for their hostility to democracy and their responsibility for encouraging the rebellion. *The Selected Writings of William Lyon Mackenzie* (Toronto, 1960), edited by Margaret Fairloy, is a useful compilation, even if there is an unbalanced emphasis, in the selections chosen and the editor's commentaries, on the rational Mackenzie. The *Mackenzie-Lindsey Papers* in the Public Archives of Ontario contain many letters, memoranda, and newspaper clippings. They were indexed by Mackenzie.

Contemporary writings that offered background, anecdotes, and quotations for this study of Mackenzie are Samuel Thompson, *Reminiscences of a Canadian Pioneer for the Last Fifty Years (1833-1883)* (Toronto, 1884; reprinted Toronto, 1968); Sir Francis Bond Head, **A Narrative* (London, 1839), which was edited by S.F. Wise and reprinted in 1969; *The Journals of Mary O'Brien: 1828-1838* (which can be read in manuscript in the Public Archives of Ontario), edited by Aubrey Saunders Miller (Toronto, 1968); the many revealing documents collected in *The Town of York, 1793-1815* (Toronto, 1962) and *The Town of York, 1815-1834* (Toronto, 1966), edited by Edith Firth for the Champlain Society; W.A. Langton (editor), *Early Days in Upper Canada: Letters of John Langton from the Backwoods of Upper Canada* and the Audit Office of the Province of Canada (Toronto, 1926); Edward A. Talbot, Five Years' Residence in the Canadas (2 vols, London, 1824); John Webster Grant (editor), *Salvation! O the Joyful Sound: The Selected Writings of John Carroll (Toronto, 1967). Interesting nineteenth-century historical works that repay study are: Henry Scadding, Toronto of Old (Toronto, 1873), abridged and edited by F.H. Armstrong (Toronto, 1966); Robina and Kathleen Lizars, Humours of '37, Grave and Grim: Rebellion Time in the Canadas (Toronto, 1897); and Mary Agnes FitzGibbon, *A Veteran of 1812: The Life of James FitzGibbon (Toronto, 1894; paperback reprint 1970).

Valuable modern studies of the Mackenzie period in Upper Canada are Aileen Dunham, *Political Unrest in Upper Canada, 1815-1836 (Toronto, 1927; paperback edition, Toronto, 1963); Gerald M. Craig, Upper Canada: The Formative Years 1784-1841 (Toronto, 1963); an unpublished thesis for the University of Toronto by F.H. Armstrong, Toronto in Transition: The Emergence of a City, 1828-1838 (1965); and David W.C. Earl, *The Family Compact: Aristocracy or Oligarchy? (Toronto, 1967). (An earlier study of this subject—W. Stewart Wallace, The Family Compact: A Chronicle of Rebellion in Upper Canada (Toronto, 1915)—is also useful.) E.C. Guillet, *Early Life in Upper Canada (Toronto, 1933), contains much interesting social history.

Ten scholarly articles are of considerable interest. In Ontario History: John Muggeridge, "John Rolph: A Reluctant Rebel", No. 4, 1959; Eric Jackson, "The Organization of Upper Canadian Reformers, 1818-1867", No. 2, 1961; F.H. Armstrong, "York Riots of 1832", No. 2, 1963; John S. Moir, "Mr Mackenzie's Secret Reporter", No. 4, 1963; John Ireland, "Andrew Drew: The Man Who Burned the Caroline", No. 3, 1967; Lillian Gates, "W.L. Mackenzie's Volunteer and the First Parliament of United Canada", No. 3, 1967; F.H. Armstrong, "Reformer as Capitalist: William Lyon Mackenzie and the Printers' Strike of 1836", No. 3, 1967. In the Canadian Historical Review: Lillian Gates, "The Decided Policy of William Lyon Mackenzie", Vol. 40, No. 3, 1959; F.H. Armstrong, "William Lyon Mackenzie, First Mayor of Toronto: A Study of a Critic in Power", Vol. 48, No. 4, 1967. F.H. Armstrong is also the author of a useful description of early Toronto, called "Toronto in 1834", which appeared in the Canadian Geographer, Vol. 10, No. 3, 1966.

Index